Flourish is more than a title of a book. In one word, it is a promise of what can and will happen IF . . . you are planted in the house of the Lord. My friend Michael Turner is a living epistle of this book, and that is why the words he has penned have transformational power to bring wholeness to anyone who reads it.

—Keith Craft

Lead Pastor of Elevate Life Church, Best-Selling author, Keith Craft Masterminds, Think Coach

Everyone wants to fulfill their special calling and live life in that sweet spot between success and happiness. Michael Turner knows the way because he's lived it. He turned his life completely around when he found that perfect place to get planted. That place is waiting for each of us . . . Where God designed us to "Flourish!"

—David Crank

Author, Speaker, Senior Pastor of FaithChurch.com

Everyone changes; few grow. Many people expect growth but are not planted in the proper soil that contributes to healthy development. Michael has provided a great resource to give direction and clarity to help you know the key steps to take for you to flourish beyond what you've ever thought possible. God's will is for you to grow, so use this as a manual to see the growth you've been longing for your entire life.

—Shaun Nepsted

Author, Founder/Lead Pastor of Fellowship Church

Michael writes from a place of proven experience. His very life is a demonstration of what it means to flourish. Get ready to be equipped and empowered to flourish like never before!

—Bishop Dale C. Bronner
Founder/Senior Pastor Word of Faith Family Worship Cathedral
Atlanta, Georgia

Flourish! What picture comes to your mind? I think of something or someone healthy, growing, blossoming, thriving, increasing, and even influencing. My good friend Michael Turner's book *Flourish* will help you do just that—flourish in every area of your life. You'll get this book for all you love and want to flourish with you.

—Dr. Samuel R. Chand, Leadership Consultant and Author of
Cracking Your Church's Culture Code (www.samchand.com)

Join Pastor Michael Turner as he takes you on a journey into God's grand design for man. Perfected faith is mature faith. Sometimes we stop short of everything God created us to be. This book reveals a roadmap of how God moves us from one season to the next until we find ourselves "FLOURISHING!"

—Ron Carpenter
Author, Pastor of Redemption Church

Michael Turner has made it his life's mission to help men and women find their purpose and succeed. In his book, *Flourish*, you will learn the principles necessary to do just that. As a friend of more than twenty-five years, I have witnessed Michael walk out these truths in his life, and I believe they will empower you as well.

—Real Talk Kim
Pastor, Author, Speaker, Coach and Social Media Influencer

FLOURISH

Finding your place for wholeness and fulfillment

MICHAEL TURNER

AVAIL

For foreign and subsidiary rights, contact the author.

Cover design by: Eric Powell
Cover Photo by: Andrew van Tilborgh

ISBN: 978-1-957369-23-5   1 2 3 4 5 6 7 8 9 10

Printed in the United States of America

Dedication

I want to dedicate this book to the woman who raised me, loved me unconditionally, took me to the house of God, and who interceded for me when I was far from God . . . my mother, Nancy Adams. Thank you, Mom, for all your love and sacrifice that helped me become who I am today. I wouldn't be here if it weren't for you. I honor you and love you so much!

CONTENTS

ACKNOWLEDGEMENTS

I want to thank my wife, Charla, who is God's amazing grace gift to me, for always saying yes to what God puts into my heart for His kingdom. Thank you for loving me and God's house like you do! I want to thank my three amazing children—Micha, Presley, and Madelyn—for loving and honoring me, doing kingdom as a family, and following me as I follow Christ. Lastly, I owe much love and gratitude to our incredible staff, leadership, and dream team at Turning Point Church that makes the vision a reality.

INTRODUCTION

'll never forget the day our first son Micha was born. Like any first-time dad, I was a nervous wreck, pulling the car around to the front of the hospital as one of the nurses pushed a wheelchair containing my wife, Charla, with our son tightly wrapped up in her arms. As I arrived at the front of the hospital, I jumped out to put my son in his car seat, checking every strap and latch over and over again as if I were preparing him for a flight around the moon—which, the more I think about it, is really quite funny based on how slowly I drove home that day.

As a new father, I wanted to do everything just right. From the warming of Micha's bottles to the diapers I mustered up enough courage to help my wife change, I can remember how important it was for me to be the best father I could be—not just for my son but, if I can be honest, for me personally as well—something I'll share more about in this book. Charla and I have been blessed not just to have one child, but three, and

11

one thing is for certain: each ride home from the hospital got faster and faster! It's amazing how parents suddenly become experts after their second or third child is born.

Well, if Charla and I thought we were pros at birthing our children (a process every man probably loves a lot more than his wife), watching each of them grow was something for which we could never have been prepared enough. From infants to toddlers, first steps to first days of school, Micha, Presley and Madelyn seemed like they grew overnight and were insisting on doing so as fast as they could. Whenever someone would ask them what their age or grade level was, it was never just, "I'm six," or, "I'm in sixth grade." It was more like, "I'm six-and-a-half," or, "I'm almost in seventh grade." No matter how many pictures or videos we as parents take in hopes of pausing and memorializing each of our children's moments and milestones, they always seem ready to grow and move on to something new.

One thing we all have in common, no matter our differences in age and backgrounds, is growth. From the time we were born, you and I grew naturally in age and in size, but when it came to our emotions, relationships, professions, and our finances, that growth was not automatic. We all have friends and coworkers whose birthdates may say one thing, but their personal maturity levels and character say another. I share with my children quite often that just because people have grown UP, it doesn't necessarily mean that they have grown ON. Even for those of us who call ourselves believers or Christ-followers, in order for our faith in God to grow, it takes a great deal of effort, commitment, and intentionality. The truth is all of us are growing in some way or another; however, I am a firm believer that not all growth is equal, which is why I believe this book is so important.

Just because people have grown UP, it doesn't necessarily mean that they have grown ON.

GROWTH REDEFINED

There are a variety of definitions for the word growth. Some define it as a gradual increase in size or a particular stage of one's development. However, years ago, I came across a synonym for the word growth that captured my attention almost immediately. In my opinion, this word not only helped redefine for me what growth was—it also defined how to grow well.

That word was FLOURISH.

According to the *Merriam-Webster Dictionary*, the word flourish means "to grow luxuriantly," "to achieve success," and to "prosper." To flourish also means "to reach the height of influence" and to "thrive."[1] I absolutely love these definitions of growth because they describe what I believe we all want out of life. All of us have an innate desire to live a successful and prosperous life in which we are thriving in everything

---

1 "Flourish Definition & Meaning," *Merriam-Webster*, https://www.merriam-webster.com/dictionary/flourish.

we set our hearts and minds to do. I mean, who doesn't want a thriving relationship or marriage? A thriving family or profession? A thriving bank account—you know, the kind you don't have to pray over every time you're at the checkout counter? Believe it or not, these are not just things that you and I want for our lives, but they are things that God wants for us to have as well.

In fact, God created you and me to flourish. We were designed by Him to live a life by design, not by default. But it was by default that I lived most of my life. I was aiming at nothing and hitting it every single time. A high school dropout, who later became a college dropout, who then almost dropped out of life due to my addiction to drugs and alcohol. These destructive, addictive habits had me discouraged constantly and sinking into a pain-filled world of darkness. As I said earlier, growth is not automatic, and the negative things in our lives that may be causing strife, anger, and bitterness can grow into cancerous diseases if we're not careful. I had grown tired of living this kind of life—so at the age of twenty-four, I decided to try something different, something that changed the trajectory of my life.

I surrendered my life to Christ and was planted in the house of God.

In Psalm 92:12-13 (NIV), you will find these words: "The righteous will flourish like a palm tree, they will grow like a cedar of Lebanon, planted in the house of the LORD, they will flourish in the courts of our God." I am confident that God's original plan for us to flourish, to grow luxuriantly, and to thrive in every area of our lives is realized when we are planted in the house of God. The truth is we are all planted somewhere in our lives. Some of us are planted in our jobs, consumed with making ends meet. Some of us are planted in our relationships, hoping that their companionship will fill up the loneliness that we often carry around with us each and every day. However, I believe that we will never flourish and see good things happen in our lives the way God intended until we are planted in the right thing and in the right place. And for me, that right thing and right place was the house of God.

Now, I know that today's culture and society has a great deal to say about the house of God—what many also describe as the local church. But the house of God (the local church) is not a building; it is the dwelling place of God, where we can connect with His presence and His people, so we can fulfill His purpose. It is the place where we can discover just how God desires for us to flourish, excel, and reach our fullest potential in life. The house of God changed my life completely—and I am confident, whether you are new to following Christ or have been doing so for a while, the house of God can change your life too, once you firmly plant yourself within it.

If you feel as though you were made for more and have grown tired with the place you find yourself living in right now, then this book was written just for you! Let's take a journey together and discover just how to flourish and fulfill the great calling that God has for our lives.

CHAPTER 1

MADE FOR MORE

sn't it amazing the things in life we so quickly forget and the things we will always remember? I can remember, a few years after my parents divorced, going to church for the very first time with my mother. I must have been eight or nine years old at that time. I can remember standing next to her on top of the pew, trying to see over the sea of heads in front of me. After just a few songs of worship, I was instantly hooked. Every chance I could, I would beg my mom to take me to church:

- ➤ Sunday morning worship.
- ➤ Sunday school.
- ➤ Back again for Sunday night worship.
- ➤ Wednesday night Bible study.

I just loved it all. Probably because it was the one place for us that felt like home. You see, my mother was raised in extreme poverty in what was one of the poorest areas in Atlanta. She had a father who abused alcohol and, consequently, abused her mother and the entire family. He later abandoned her and her five siblings to be raised by a single mom. And when she became a single mom herself, she made a conscious decision that something had to change. By committing herself to God and becoming a champion for the local church, my mother was modeling for me as a young boy that you may not have come from a great family, but a great family could still come from you.

You may not have come from a great family, but a great family could still come from you.

Despite her circumstances and the faulty starting blocks she knew she and my father had given me, she was determined for me to know early on that I was made for more. And you know what? You were made for more too!

In Genesis 1:31, we read of a God who created the heavens and the earth and everything in them. From the fish and the birds to the plants and trees, God uniquely designed and created each thing with the potential to contain and produce new life from within it. In the heavens, the stars were contained. In the soil, the plants were contained. And in the water, fish were contained. Everything that God created in Genesis 1 was given the ability to reproduce after itself. And the same is true for you and me.

When God created Adam, He did so after His likeness and placed within him the ability to contain and produce life. Eve was created from Adam, and both were given a unique calling by God to do something important with the seeds of greatness He had placed inside of them. What exactly was this calling, you ask? It's the same calling that He has given you and me today to chase after.

BE FRUITFUL AND MULTIPLY

In Genesis 1:28 (NLT), just before He planned to rest from all of His work, God told Adam (and Eve) to be "fruitful and multiply." Now, when I first became a Christian, I immediately thought that God was just telling them to go and make lots of babies, but that's not what He was talking about. What God was referring to was that Adam and Eve take dominion over everything He created and expand it throughout the earth for His glory. At the very beginning of time, God's sole desire was to create a family that would be marked by His name and resemblance—one that could build and receive generational blessings.

Perhaps that's why Satan, our enemy and foe, decided to appear to Adam and Eve in Genesis 3 and convince them to reject and rebel against God. Showing up to them as the snake he really is, he knew then, just as he does today, that if you and I ever fully understood God's purpose for us to be fruitful and multiply, there would be nothing he could do to stop us. Knowing that we can *be, do,* and *have* whatever God has purposed for us drives him crazy. In fact, Satan's sole desire since God cast him out of heaven has been to bring chaos to our world, fragment it, and separate God's people from Him; whereas God's sole desire is to redeem mankind and empower them for eternal greatness.

Repeat these words after me: *Be fruitful and multiply.*

I've always found it interesting that, when God created Adam and Eve and gave them this incredible call and purpose, He did so in the midst of a garden. Now, while I've never been much for gardening—I've probably killed far more plants than I care to admit—I do know that for any garden to be fruitful and produce well, it requires several things. It requires good soil, as well as an adequate supply of water and sunlight. But no matter how good the soil is, and no matter the amount of water and sun, in order for a garden to be fruitful, it requires plowing. I'm not sure if you've ever had to plow through the ground, pull weeds, or remove any debris or pests that are known to choke out the seeds you're wanting to plant, but trust me when I tell you it takes a lot of hard work.

The truth is, plowing where we ultimately desire to be fruitful is not an easy thing to do.

The truth is, plowing where we ultimately desire to be fruitful is not an easy thing to do.

One garden that may be the most difficult for us to plow—that is also often the place we doubt will ever produce fruit—is our minds. I love what Henry Ford, American automobile inventor and founder of one the world's most renown companies, once said about our minds, and particularly, the way you and I think: "Whether you think you can or whether you think you can't, you are right."

In Proverbs 23:7 (KJV), King Solomon, one of the wisest persons who ever lived, provided a similar thought nearly three thousand years before Ford did: "For as he thinketh in his heart, so *is* he." How you and I think determines how we believe, what we do, and what we will have in our lives. As believers, sometimes it's hard for us to understand that most of the results we are experiencing right now are not a matter of our praying, but rather a matter of our thinking. For us to live the kind of fruitful lives God has planned for us, we have to begin changing the way we think about ourselves, no matter how difficult our past.

The greatest gift we can give to others is a healthy version of ourselves.

The greatest gift we can give to others is a healthy version of ourselves. And we are at our healthiest when we are willing to stretch and grow into the person God is calling us to be. No matter what our lives may look like today, we have to have a growth mindset, be unafraid to begin doing things differently, and refuse to settle for what is easy. It would have been easy for my mother to give up on her future after my father and she divorced. Instead, she refused to take the path of least resistance. She worked hard and excelled at her place of employment, working her way into upper-level management. She worked a lot of overtime, so we could have a better life, and she became a faithful giver to the house of God.

When I found myself lying in an emergency room hospital bed after a three-day drinking and drug binge, the easiest thing for me to do was to give up on myself and end my life. Instead, I began remembering the songs I used to sing while in church, the prayers I used to pray while in church, as well as those that were prayed over me. I remembered hearing messages about a God whose love for me was so great that, even when I probably deserved His judgement, His grace and mercy were still mine for the asking. When I came face to face with the God of my youth and acknowledged how I was rebelling against Him and His love for me, He was quick to remind me that I was still His child, and my shortcomings would do nothing to change that fact.

Never in my wildest dreams would I have believed that at the age of fifty-two, I would be blessed with the wife and three kids I have today. If you were to tell me that I, one day, would be pastoring one of the greatest churches in all of South Atlanta, I would have looked at you cross-eyed. God has blown my mind time and time again—not because of me, but because of what He wanted to do through me.

What thoughts are you wrestling with today about yourself? What is it about your past that is causing you to think that you'll never be fruitful or that you weren't made for more than what you see today? Friends, you may not believe this, but there is legacy inside of you. And, no, that was not a typo.

LEGACY-MINDED

Everything that God desires to do for us is never really about us but rather about what He desires to do *through* us. There is a story God is writing about you that is bigger than you. It is important to know, once and for all, that God never placed you on this earth to be good but to do good. You were not just saved from something, but you were saved to do something. As Christians, it is so easy for us to mirror so many of the world's values concerning our lives and our purposes. We have all been guilty, one time or another, of being more focused on doing a hobby, purchasing a car, or building a career than we were on expanding God's kingdom and leaving a legacy that would make Him smile.

Everywhere you look today, whether you are scrolling through your phone or via your remote, it seems like everyone has become best friends with what I like to call the *Me Monster*. Perhaps more frightening than any Halloween movie we've seen, this monster literally feeds on our selfish nature. It is driven by the lust of our flesh and how consumed we all can become with wanting the world to know who we are instead of *whose* we are. Nothing points this out more clearly than 1 John 2:16 (NLT): "For the world offers only a craving for physical pleasure, a craving for everything we see, and pride in our achievements and possessions. These are not from the Father, but are from the world."

As children of God, called to be fruitful and multiply, we have to become legacy-minded when it comes to the things we say and do and the places we choose to go to spend our time. That word legacy literally means to be able to pass something of worth down to someone else. Just as land and riches can be passed down from one generation to the next, the same is true with the values we uphold as believers. What we believe matters. And what we put into practice matters even more.

> ## What we believe matters. And what we put into practice matters even more.

As a first-generation pastor, knowing that I may not have been on the receiving end of a great legacy but that I am responsible for leaving one for my kids has been something that has inspired me more than anything else. From the time our children were able to walk into church, just as I did with my mother when I was their age, Charla and I were determined that they would serve in some capacity, great or small. From singing on stage to giving food to those in need, each of our kids learned early on that their lives are not their own, but they were placed on this earth to be a blessing to others. Every Sunday, when I see them serving and giving in our church, I am reminded that legacy is really not about what you build but who you are raising up.

Legacy is really not about what you build but who you are raising up.

Each of us has been given a legacy to live and a legacy to leave behind, and it begins by embracing the belief that we were made for more. God has never changed His mind concerning His children and their purpose. What He asked Adam and Eve to do in the garden He is still asking you and me to do today. The time has come for us to be fruitful and multiply—to subdue the earth with His glory for the renown of His name. If I'm coming off like a broken record (be fruitful and multiply . . . you were made for more . . . it's time to leave a legacy), I make no apologies. Perhaps it's because our Heavenly Father has been doing the same thing far longer than I have: "He is the faithful God who keeps His covenant for a thousand generations and lavishes His unfailing love on those who love Him and obey His commands" (Deuteronomy 7:9, NLT).

To know that our God wants to lavish you and me with His love ought to excite you! I've been reading that passage of scripture for over twenty years, and I still get excited about it! And to know that the love of God is unfailing, even when I have failed Him time and time again, is just something I will never understand. This is why I believe it is so important for you and me to get planted in the house of God.

For me personally, His house has in many ways felt like *holy ground*. Let me explain why.

CHAPTER 2
HOLY GROUND

shared in the introduction of this book a passage of scripture that was, in many ways, the primary inspiration behind this book on flourishing. The scripture was written by a man by the name of David who, if there were ever a poster child for a "church boy," would have definitely fit the bill. Here is that scripture again, found in Psalm 92:12 (NLT): "The righteous will flourish like a palm tree, they will grow like a cedar of Lebanon, planted in the house of the LORD, they will flourish in the courts of our God."

The Holy Spirit inspired David to beautifully pen and describe that being planted in the house of God was one of the most important keys to our flourishing in our lives. I often wondered why, as someone who spent a large majority of his youth outside looking after his father's sheep, David found the house of God so important.

The truth is that we are all hardwired to instinctively desire a house. It doesn't matter if that house is made out of mud and straw, brick or stucco—we all we all desire to be covered. A house is far more than a building that covers our heads; a house is where most of what we believe and hold fast to in life is first taught. Who we are, our likes and dislikes, are often first discovered inside of a house. And our sense of family, whether it be bad or good, can become a permanent image in our minds based upon what went on inside the walls of our houses while we were young. I know it may sound cliché, but home can truly be where the heart is.

Well, the house of God is where the heart of God is. It is His dwelling place. It is not just a building with stained glass windows or one with a steeple and a cross on top of it. In fact, the house of God cannot be confined or limited to a physical address, as we serve a God who is described as "omnipresent." He has the ability to be wherever His people choose to gather. Religion has taught you that the building itself, (the brick, the mortar, the metal, and the wood) is what is sacred and holy, but that is not what I believe. What makes the house of God a holy place is that it is where God chooses to provide us with His presence. Everywhere His presence resides becomes holy ground.

Everywhere His presence resides becomes holy ground.

I want to go back to Adam and Eve for just a second because they were blessed with the opportunity to experience the very first house of God, also known as the Garden of Eden. I find it interesting that this garden—one that was perfectly designed by God Himself—somehow still became a place where our enemy was able to sneak in. In just the first three chapters of the Bible, Adam and Eve went from communing with God and His creation to having to deal with Satan.

It's no secret: Satan despises God. And he despises the thing that God loves most: His family.

I used to wonder how in the world someone like this could enter such a perfect place. I then discovered that Satan was an angel whom many theologians believe was a worship leader in heaven—and who, out of his own pride and lust to be more than he was, influenced nearly a third of all of the angels in heaven to rebel against God. Can you imagine the audacity necessary to cause someone to rebel against God in His own house? Well, if someone was capable of being tossed out of heaven, it's no wonder that he found a way to slide into the house of God. He is determined to do whatever he needs to do to cause division between us and God. He is a master deceiver and what the Bible calls a "father of lies."[2]

It makes me sick to my stomach just writing about him, so let me get us through this last part, so we can talk about something far more important which is the house of God. When Satan approached Adam and Eve, he immediately began to slander God and to convince Adam and Eve to believe a lie about Him and the things He had spoken to them. Satan had one goal which was to deceive Adam and Eve to believe they can do things their way—to redefine God's Word.

I've been in full-time ministry for twenty-five years now; nineteen of those I've served as the pastor of my church. Throughout all of those years of serving God's people, I have discovered that Satan is still up to the same old games. He has no new tricks. He is still using gossip, slander, and lies to separate God's people and divide them against Him and the dwelling place He has created for them—the very place in which they're meant to be planted.

When Adam and Eve bought into the lie Satan sold them, it ultimately caused death to enter into the world—not just death in the form of ceasing to live but death as it relates to separation from God and the holy ground He had established for us to live in. What was supposed to be a place with unhindered fellowship and access—a place in which we would spend our days being fruitful and multiplying His purpose in the earth—became a place Adam and Eve were forced to leave. However, I am thankful God did not choose to leave them. Before they left His

2 John 8:44 (NLT)

house, God devised a masterful plan to not only redeem them but also to redeem anyone else who would find themselves separated from His presence.

So what was His plan? Check out what God says in Genesis 3:15 (NLT): "And I will cause hostility between you and the woman, and between your offspring and her offspring. He will strike your head, and you will strike his heel."

In this passage, God prophesied thousands of years in advance the coming of His Son, Jesus Christ. When Jesus died on the cross for our sins, He did not only crush the head of Satan—He also placed Satan under our feet. Through the sacrifice of Christ, God reclaimed authority over the earth and made certain, once and for all, that His house and dwelling place would never be taken over again. The gates of hell would never prevail again against the house of God. Even when the enemy of our souls tries to strip our dignity, just as He did with Adam and Eve, we can have confidence that God's house and His family have been fully restored.

When Adam and Eve left the garden, God chose to sacrifice an animal and shed its blood in an effort to cover their nakedness that day. God has always been wanting to cover His children, and while many of us are still trying to cover ourselves, the best covering we will ever obtain is when we are planted again in God's house. His house is the only soil through which we can truly flourish.

> ## His house is the only soil through which we can truly flourish.

If I can place my gardener hat on again for just one moment, it is so important for us to know that the soil we're planted in matters. You can have top-quality seed, but if the soil is no good, nothing will grow from it. The seeds of greatness that are inside of you must be planted in soil that is fertile and holy, which is why I believe that God's house is, in fact, holy ground. It is on this ground that you and I are able to fulfill the high calling of God in Christ Jesus. Earlier, I wrote that David was pretty passionate about God's house, but it was Jesus who gave His very life for it.

Both David and Jesus, who providentially share the same royal blood-line, described themselves as "consumed" with the house of God.[3] Their passion to see God's house honored and revered is something we all, as God's sons and daughters, ought to share. As the loving Father that He is, God wants His house full of those who love Him—those He has called and given His purpose to.

And yet, I know for some of you reading this, that word house does not always resonate well. Perhaps, just like me, the absence of a father at home has made you cautious about receiving love from a God who describes Himself as a father. Or just like me—the mistakes you've made

---

3 Psalm 69:9; John 2:17 (NLT)

in life have you wondering if you could ever be welcomed inside of someone's home. Well, think again.

COME HOME

In Luke 15, Jesus shared a parable with His disciples about a young man who is often referred to as "the prodigal son." After being raised in what seemed to be a wealthy home alongside his older brother, Jesus said that one day, the younger son approached his father with what was, in those days, a proposal few would dare to make: "The younger son told his father, 'I want my share of your estate now before you die.' So his father agreed to divide his wealth between his sons" (v. 12, NLT).

Before we read over the rest of this parable, can you imagine being a father and hearing that request from one of your sons?

"Hey, Dad, it looks to me like you're not dying fast enough. Would you mind giving me my money now, please?"

I don't know what I would have reached for faster if one of my sons asked me that: some tissues or my belt . . . but let's continue:

Not long after that, the younger son got together all he had, set off for a distant country and there squandered his wealth in wild living. After he had spent everything, there was a severe famine in that whole country, and he began to be in need. So he went and hired himself out to a citizen of that country, who sent him to his fields to feed pigs. He longed to fill his stomach with the pods that the pigs were eating, but no one gave him anything. —vv. 13-16 (NIV)

In what may have been a little over a week according to some translations, this young man went from flourishing in the house of his father to scrounging up scraps in a pen of pigs. What in the world was a prince doing lying around with pigs? Nothing can demoralize us and strip us of our dignities like pride and selfishness. Just like Adam and Eve were stripped of their rightful place when deceived by the enemy's lies, this young man found himself begging for provision when he'd once enjoyed an ample supply. While the main characters of these stories are different, the result is still the same: Whenever we remove ourselves from God's house, we will cease from flourishing.

Whenever we remove ourselves from God's house, we will cease from flourishing.

If, today, you can identify with this young man—if it seems like lately, you've been living a messy, piglike life—I want you to know there is still hope for you. I have been where you've been; it felt as though there were nothing I could do to dig myself out of the holes I'd made. But after reading this next verse one day, I realized that God was not interested in my digging myself out of something but in my coming back to something. It was time to come back home.

> *When he came to his senses, he said, "How many of my father's hired servants have food to spare, and here I am starving to death! I will set out and go back to my father and say to him: "Father, I have sinned against heaven and against you. I am no longer worthy to be called your son; make me like one of your hired servants." So he got up and went to his father. But while he was still a long way off, his father saw him and was filled with compassion for him; he ran to his son, threw his arms around him and kissed him.* —Luke 15:17-20 (NIV)

This younger son made a choice that every lost son and daughter can make when they feel as though they are far from the presence of God; he came to his senses, and he went back home. Despite the mistakes he made and the things he once said, he recognized, just as you and I must do today, that planted in the house of God is where we flourish the most.

The house of God is where joy is.

The house of God is where our purpose is.

And perhaps, most importantly, it is in the house of God where our Father is.

A Father who loves us and is always willing to welcome us back home.

I love this story of the prodigal son because as soon as he turned back to his father, the father went to him. There was no hesitation. He didn't need to take a bath before receiving a hug from his father. His father immediately gave him a ring and a robe, which signified to everyone watching, that he was a son of the king. While the son was determined to remind his father about his shortcomings, the father was more interested in reminding him of his inheritance.

That's what flourishing in God's house is all about. It's about inheritance. Legacy. Purpose.

You have a purpose in God's house. You do not have to wait to get to heaven to discover your purpose. The minute you decide to return to God and get planted in His house, you will begin to flourish. No matter what you've done, there is always room in God's house for you. Remember: God's house is not about entering into a building. It is about belonging to a family.

Now that we know how important it is to be planted in God's house and that we were made for far more than what the enemy may have been whispering to us in the past, I want to spend a little time sharing with you what the house of God is actually made up of.

IT COMES IN THREES

The first time the phrase "house of God" is ever mentioned in the Bible is in Genesis 28. Interestingly enough, this came about as a result of a dream. Jacob, the grandson of Abraham—whom the Bible describes as the father of "many nations"—had fallen asleep in a place called Luz. While asleep, he began to dream about a stairway to heaven. Angels were ascending and descending down this ladder-like stairway from earth to heaven. Although the Bible does not talk about how long Jacob was asleep, the Bible is very clear about what he did when he woke up:

> Then Jacob awoke from his sleep and said, "Surely the LORD is in this place, and I wasn't even aware of it!" But he was also afraid and said, "What an awesome place this is! It is none other than the house of God, the very gateway to heaven!" The next morning Jacob got up very early. He took the stone he had rested his head against, and he set it upright as a memorial pillar. Then he poured olive oil over it. He named that place Bethel (which means house of God), although it was previously called Luz. —Genesis 28:16-19 (NLT)

Why did Jacob call the place where he had this dream "Bethel," which is translated to mean the "house of God?" I believe it was because he experienced the full reality of God's presence. Bethel is a combination of two separate words: *Beth* (which means "house") and *El* (which is the Hebrew name for God). Perhaps that's why God chose, thousands of years later, to select Bethlehem (which means "the house of bread") as the birthplace of His Son, Jesus Christ. God always finds a way to use His house for His glory.

In Jacob's dream that day, God presented Himself to Jacob, affirmed who He was, and also affirmed what Jacob's purpose was to be from that day forward. For Jacob, the place where he went to sleep that night became holy ground. It became a dwelling place where he was able to connect with God's presence and be reminded about His people so that he could fulfill His purpose in the earth.

That is why I believe that there are three elements to God's house. They are:

1) His Presence.
2) His People.
3) His Purpose.

It is through these three elements that we connect best with God. The house of God is the only place where these three things exist at the same time. It's why giving our lives is worth championing the mission of the church. The church was not placed on earth by God to give us a weekly show; it is a flow and atmosphere where He can connect and commune with us fully.

When the presence, people, and purpose of God come together, it is powerful to witness. It's much like what scientists refer to as "synergy." Whenever two or more elements come together, this synergy can cause something to be more than what it was. The same is true for the house of God. When we gather together on holy ground, we are seizing the opportunity to be connected with God in community with others, combining our God-given potential and purpose to change the world.

That is one of my greatest prayers behind this book: that you will, in fact, change the world. As a pastor, I get to see firsthand what happens when the children of God begin to flourish. There is nothing quite like seeing the seeds of greatness inside of a person be *discovered, developed, and deployed* the way God has destined them to be. No matter what pigpen they may have found themselves in—whether they have spent years falling asleep with unfulfilled purpose in a place called Luz—I am grateful that I have the opportunity to remind people that the house of God is still available to them.

There is still room in God's house.

There is still grace in God's house.

Every day I get up, I get excited about a place in which His presence, His people, and His purpose are things I no longer have to run from but that I can run *to*. It's no wonder David, who had more low moments in life than all of us put together, wrote these amazing words in Psalm 122:1 (NLT): "I was glad when they said to me, 'Let us go into the house of the LORD.'"

As we continue to learn more about how to flourish within each element of God's house, I hope the same gladness David felt is one you will experience, too. Who's ready to go?

THE PRESENCE OF GOD

CHAPTER 3

THERE'S NO PLACE LIKE HOME

While I didn't realize it at the time, growing up as a young boy without the presence of a father in the house was devastating. I vividly remember the day he left my mother—I remember wondering why he wouldn't fight to stay home with her or, at the least, fight to stay home for me. It took several years for me to finally realize that he was fighting many other things back then—that the idea of staying home with us probably felt impossible. But the idea of a father always fighting and pursuing his children with relentless love is what I believe a healthy home should always be built upon, which is probably why I am so very passionate about the house of God.

> # We, as God's children, will never be orphans because we have a Father who will never give up on us and is always fighting for us.

The first element that makes up the house of God is the presence of a father—and not just any father, but a faithful, everlasting Father who will never leave us or abandon us. We, as God's children, will never be orphans because we have a Father who will never give up on us and is always fighting for us: fighting for our focus and fighting for our devotion. You don't have to be from Kansas or from a land called Oz to know that, when a good father is present, there really is no place like home!

Psalm 26:8 (ESV) says, "O Lord, I love the habitation of your house and the place where your glory dwells." Why did David write, "I love the habitation of your HOUSE"? Because it's the place where His glory dwells, forever and always. Flourishing in the house begins with being awakened to the access we now have to the very presence of God—wherever we go, God's presence and house are the same. Now, even more than David, we have opportunity through the blood of Jesus to come boldly into God's presence and know that we will always be welcomed because we are His family.

God wants us to be passionate about the house. He wants us planted in the house. Psalm 92:13 (NLT) says, "For they are transplanted to the LORD's own house. They flourish in the courts of our God." Our faithful Father God fights for us and never gives up. He fights our enemies, and He fights for our focus, our devotion. You can imagine that, when I first began to follow Christ, it was a process for me to understand God's love as a Father: that He was full of overwhelming love and grace. It took some time before I was able to understand and receive that kind of love. It was and still is good news that His presence will never leave me or forsake me. Hebrews 13:5 (NLT) says, "For God has said, 'I will never fail you. I will never abandon you.'" In Christ, that promise is for you, too!

Some fear that God will leave them or abandon them if they are not good boys and girls, but that's not how our good Father is. When we realize that, as sons and daughters, we are loved based not on our behavior but on our birthright, we can live free from the fear that Daddy God will leave us or not love us. Many times, people stay away from the house because they think Dad (God) left home and left them behind for better things—better *kids*. They assume he's mad at them, done with them . . . but not this Dad.

Every time we come home, we can be assured that He will be there waiting for us with love, grace, and mercy. We see that in Luke 15 when the prodigal son comes home. His father was waiting and ran to him with kisses, love, restoration, and celebration.

As a child of God, I have access. Ever since my children were little, they've known that when I was in the house, they had access to me, no matter where I was. If I was working, studying, doing finances, or whatever, they had access to my presence. They still do. It is the same with God and His presence. This is why we, like David, should love the habitation of God's house. It's why we can say, "I love my church." Why? It's God's house, filled with the presence, the people, and the purpose of God. It's the place of habitation, the dwelling place, of *Yahweh—Abba*, Daddy.

When I was younger and my dad and mom were separated, Dad would come over to visit. I loved it and didn't want him to leave. In fact, he was with me this past week—for five days. We spent time with him every day; the kids, Charla, and I talked, ate, laughed, and shared stories of the past with him. He was in the house, and it was a habitation for five days.

After he experienced our church for the first time, he was amazed, honored, and so proud. He expressed this to me as I was taking him back home. When I dropped him off, I hugged him, told him I loved him, and that I was so grateful for his visit with us. We had grown closer because of it. As I was walking back to my car, I unexpectedly started to cry as many emotions flooded over me.

First, I was so grateful to God for giving us this time and for bringing healing from years of pain and absence. Then, I thought of all the years we could have shared together, but that were now out of reach. Then, I realized I didn't want the visit to end—I guess a part of me wanted him to stay. As a son longing for the habitation of his father, I believe this is how we should be towards our God. People talk about a visitation from God—I don't want just a visitation. I want Him to stay! I want a habitation in which His presence and glory dwell—where we talk, laugh, connect, and dream about the future together. May we learn the treasure of abiding in Him—loving, seeking, and dwelling in the habitation of his house!

Psalm 91:1 (NKJV) says, "He who dwells in the secret place of the Most High, shall abide under the shadow of the Almighty." Looking at simple English, to "abide/dwell" means to "live." Where you live is the place you inhabit, take residence—it's your address, the one place you go no matter where you've been during the day. It is the place where everyone knows you can be found. A dwelling place in itself expresses permanency; the verse says they shall abide "in the shadow"—close to the one *casting* the shadow.

Many times, we visit with God. But really, He wants us to *dwell with* him, not just visit when we need something, like a child who only contacts a parent when they need something. God doesn't want to be treated like a celestial Santa Claus or genie in a bottle. In order to change this, we need a change of address. We must choose to abide in the presence of God. That's when joy comes, healing happens, fear goes, depression ceases, demons flee, and victory is obtained.

John 15:5 (NKJV) says, "I am the vine, you are the branches. He who abides in Me, and I in him, bears much fruit; for without Me you can do nothing." If we remain in Jesus, stay connected to Jesus—His Word, His voice, His presence—we will grow in good things—in *God* things. When we control our attention, affection, and allegiance to Jesus, that's when the real fruit begins to grow.

Remember, the great calling is to "Be fruitful and multiply" (Genesis 1:28, NLT). You may even hear people try to seem spiritual by saying, "Wow, all you care about is growth!" But the more I know God and study His Word, the more I see that God cares a lot about growth! When we grow, we flourish—we thrive instead of just survive.

John 15:8 (NLT) reads, "When you produce much fruit, you are my true disciples. This brings great glory to my Father." When you produce much fruit, you give evidence that you are His. God wants us to mature, so we can reproduce! Why *wouldn't* we want to see results in our character—the way we talk, walk, and live? The time I invest with Him manifests the fruit of who I am in Him. If we change our spiritual address, we can change our lives, our habits, and what comes out of our mouths. We will experience true freedom, joy, and Christlikeness. We will flourish in family, relationships, our calling, and in our purpose. True disciples bear *much fruit*. Jesus said this is what glorifies Father God which should be the goal of our lives as God's sons and daughters.

Change is inevitable, but growth is optional. When we choose to abide in the secret place daily, practicing His presence, in His dwelling, we will grow in every good thing: relationships, soul, spirit, and purpose. We will stay connected to Him and reproduce His image in the earth.

When we abide, we take action steps of faith: we pray hard, love hard, worship hard, study hard, and work hard. It's God's grace, but we still apply diligence and give God something to work with—and people something to respect!

I do what is possible, and His presence does the impossible. This is the story of Abraham, Moses, Joshua, Ruth, David, Nehemiah, Peter, Paul . . . and you and me! As we love God, love His house, and abide in His presence, we will grow in good things. We will do the impossible. But it does require changing our minds and changing our addresses—the places we choose to dwell.

Stop dwelling on your past, your failures, your weaknesses, and where you missed it. Start dwelling in the house of God; the place where His glory dwells. You will be filled with God's glory, joy, and victorious power. God wants us to grow in His house and from His house, in the saturated, fertile soil of holy ground.

> **God wants us to grow in His house and from His house, in the saturated, fertile soil of holy ground.**

REVELATION IN THE HABITATION

John 1 tells us that God gives the right to become children of God to those who believe and accept Jesus Christ. Through faith in Jesus as the Son of God, we can be born again as a child of God.

Biology tells that it is the seed of the father that determines a child's identity, and so it is spiritually; we can never fulfill our purpose until we know who we are and whose we are.

Identity is crucial for everything that wants to fulfill its potential and purpose. Every successful business has an identity. Nike has the Swoosh and Michael Jordan. The late Steve Jobs and Macintosh have the Apple. Football teams have their slogans and mascots. Churches have mission statements and logos. Even gangs have identities with specific colors and hand signs. In the same way, identity is extremely significant to every individual who wants to fulfill his or her potential and purpose.

Fathers are instrumental in the development of our identities. Fathers have the power to affirm us and validate us. I truly believe that every child needs a father. The greatest need a child has is a father looking them in the eyes and saying, "You are my child." Every son and daughter needs to be validated. Even Jesus Christ, after He was baptized, was publicly validated by the Father before He stepped into His ministry. In Matthew 3:17 (NIV), we see God the Father validating His Son: "And a voice from heaven said, 'This is my Son, whom I love; with him I am well pleased.'" When God the Father affirmed Jesus as a Son, He was reinforcing Jesus' identity so that He would be secure in His manhood.

In Luke 4:3 (NLT), when Jesus was being tempted by Satan in the wilderness, Satan tried to get Jesus to question His identity by saying, "If you are the Son of God. . . ." I love the fact that Jesus never responded to this except with scripture because He was secure in His identity. At His baptism, His humanity was affirmed by His Father. Jesus knew who He was and whose He was—therefore, He couldn't be a victim questioning his identity as the beloved Son of God. If we are going to overcome the identity issue, we are going to need to be affirmed by our Heavenly Father as a son or daughter of the Most High God.

Not having the affirmation and touch of a father in my life caused me to be extremely insecure. I was always trying to get laughs in class which caused me to get in trouble often. It caused me to not be able to trust because of my fear of rejection or abandonment. It caused me to be critical of others, and I had a negative outlook on everything in life. Insecurity caused my heart to be full of pride—in fact, I believe that the root of pride is insecurity. Pride was first noted in the heart of Satan, and it caused his fall from heaven. Pride, at its core, is satanic. Scripture tells us that God resists the proud but gives grace to the humble. I think it's worth noting, too, that it was Satan, filled with pride, who was tempting Jesus to question His own identity—but because Jesus, as the Son of Man, had already heard the voice of His Father validating His identity, He didn't question it.

Many today struggle with insecurity. I truly believe it's because they have never been affirmed by a father. Identity issues have crippled our society in many ways. We live in a culture in which children are growing up without a godly Father to help define their identities. When good fathers, godly fathers, are removed, it tends to distort our identity—people find themselves looking to other sources in an attempt to gain an identity, even if these sources are the wrong ones.

Take gangs, for instance. Young boys and girls will turn to a dangerous, violent life, risking their own, just to try and grasp at something to identify with. These young people who turned to gang life—or left it—have clearly expressed identity as a root issue. Many of those who joined did so to find some sense of self. They are not living up to their potential; nor do they see their divine design. Many of these young men and women are simply posing to gain acceptance—a lot like Jacob posed as Esau to get his father's blessing. Isaac loved Esau more than Jacob . . . and what a profound effect it had on Jacob. Jacob was a trickster and a deceiver. He tricked his dad and his brother by posing.

Young men who are posing are trying to be someone they are not—trying to gain an identity with success in entertainment, sports, fame, or possessions. It may not be a gang that one jumps headfirst into to try and find identity; it may be fame or fortune. Sometimes men and women can believe that if they just have a large, successful ministry, it will establish their identity. For those who are trying to do this, please know that these things and accomplishments can never fulfill you. Only the affirmation of knowing who you can be in Jesus Christ can settle your identity issues so that you can flourish in the Father's house.

As you hear the Father's voice saying, You are my beloved child in whom I am well pleased, understand that you are fully known and completely loved by God. You don't have to be approved by anyone because you are already approved by God. You don't have to perform to get love or keep your position. It's not based on your behavior, but your birthright—not your performance, but your position. In Christ, you are positioned as a child of God!

You are adopted and joint-heirs with Christ according to Romans 8:15-17 (NLT):

> *So you have not received a spirit that makes you fearful slaves. Instead, you received God's Spirit when he adopted*

you as his own children. Now we call him, "Abba, Father."
For his Spirit joins with our spirit to affirm that we are God's
children. And since we are his children, we are his heirs. . . .

Being adopted in the times and Eastern culture of the New Testament was different from today's Western culture. At the time of the writing of Romans, there were three cultures: Greek, Roman, and Jewish. As a child, if you brought shame or dishonor to the family, they could divorce you, remove you from the lineage, disinherit you, and even take your last name. Not so with adopted children. Those consequences were not allowed; adoption was irrevocable! So when God says we are his adopted children in our identity through Christ, we have a reason for joy and celebration because nothing can separate us from His love or our position in His family. He is for you, not against you. Stop managing your brokenness and be whole; be healed in the name of Jesus. Believe it, receive it today, and declare that you know you are a child of God forever!

Scripture shows us another instance in which Jesus was in the house, and four guys let their paralyzed friend down through an opening they created in the roof. When He saw their faith, Jesus spoke to the disabled man's identity first, then his sin issue, and finally his need to be physically healed. Jesus not only saw the man's physical disability, He also saw his spiritual disability (sin) as well as his internal disability—his identity. I am sure this man was carrying great shame about his condition. In Jewish culture, anyone who was crippled could not enter the temple of God to worship. With this, came great shame—for men especially, who considered it a great honor to be able to enter into the temple of the living God of Israel to worship. Jesus was able to look past this man's need for physical healing and speak to his identity issue first. I am sure that he didn't feel like a son of Abraham, even though by birth he was. Notice this encounter in Mark 2:5 and 11 (NKJV): "Son, your sins are forgiven. . . . arise take up your bed, and go to your house." Jesus addressed his identity issue first. He called him "son." In essence, He was saying, "I see that you want to be physically healed, but this issue of identity is much bigger than your physical healing. Son, you are forgiven. Now, get up and take your position as a son."

I truly believe that every person needs to hear those words from Father God in the Son Jesus: "My son, my daughter, you are forgiven. Now rise up from your bed of disability, be healed, get up, and take your position as a child of God." You may never have heard those words before. Maybe you have been abandoned or rejected, never validated, but hear the voice of your Father in Heaven as He says, "My son, My daughter. . . . You don't have to be disabled or confused any longer. You are My child, you are forgiven, and you are healed. Now pick up your mat, the bed of affliction you have been laying on, and go tell your story."

The mat represented the man's past (his story), and after the miracle, it represented God's redemption. Jesus told him to pick it up and carry it, so others would see what the Lord had done for him. In our own lives, Jesus wants to give us validation as children of God, forgive us, and heal us. We in turn walk in those things with confidence as validated children who can tell their stories to others, bringing glory to the Father. The thing (the need) that may have carried you into the house of God, into His presence, is something you will overcome; you will pick it up and carry it out because it no longer has power over you.

If you don't know who you are, you don't know where your house is.

Notice that Jesus said, "Go to your house." If you don't know who you are, you don't know where your house is. As children of God, we need to know that we have become heirs of the kingdom of God. We need to know that God has a house. The scriptures teach us that we are God's house, and together, we are living stones making up one big house. In other words, the house is the body of Christ. I so love the body of Christ, the church of the living God. Some people don't like the church; they don't believe in the church, but as for me and my family, we love the church. If it hadn't been for the church or the house of God, I don't know where I would be today. It was the community of authentic Christ-followers that gathered where I went after straying for over a decade. A house represents power. Even within the American government, we see that: we have the House of Representatives, the White House, and we also have God's house! God's power flows from His house, the church.

Power always flows from a house. So, go to your house—God's house, the church. Yes, there are some flaky, phony, dead institutions called churches, but always know that there are authentic, Christ-centered,

Spirit-led, Spirit-filled churches everywhere, more than ever, all over the world. You usually find many in every city across our nation with all the church planting going on in our country. In our church, we are a part of two church planting organizations that are planting everywhere in the U.S. You can visit their websites to find one near you. The central one we are in partnership with is the Association of Related church es, also known as ARC. You can go to www.relatedchurches.com for more information. I strongly encourage you to find your house, and go to it. I know from personal experience that God will launch you into your life purpose, your kingdom purpose, with power from the local church.

We have a generation of prodigals who have never been in the Father's house, so they don't know who they are or where to go.

When you know who you are and whose you are, you know where the house is.

We discover our true identity in His presence—it is a revelation we discover in HABITATION with God.

With fatherlessness abounding in the world today, there is identity crisis and confusion. It was my story too, until I came to the house of God, where I encountered the presence of God and lay everything at the feet of Jesus. I heard my Father's voice in my Father's presence in my Father's house, and it was there that I discovered what I could do. For the first time as a son, I knew I was loved not because of what I had done but because of who I was and whose I was.

The devil knows that if a person can understand this and be validated, it brings confidence and stability to their life. Children need to feel that they are legitimate, not unwanted or illegitimate. You may not know who you are because your father never affirmed you; you may be a fully-grown adult on the outside, but on the inside, there is that little child needing the affirming voice of a loving father.

I want you to know that this is what God wants to do for you right now. You see, it is in His presence that we too can hear the Father call us a son or daughter. Like Jesus, when we hear this, we have clarity as to our value and purpose: "Son or daughter, your sins are forgiven. Daughter, your faith has made you whole. Take up your mat and walk. Go to your house!" Every son and daughter needs a house, and there is no place like the Father's house.

Yes, there has been pain, rejection, and betrayal, but make no mistake about it: God is about to flip the script. For everything the thief has done to do you that has been evil, God is about to turn it around for your good so that you, too, can realize that you are not a victim. You are a victor. You will know that there is no place like home.

CHAPTER 4

HE WANTS TO STAY (HABITATION)

I f you really enter into God's presence, you'll experience something that you didn't have when you came in.

It says in Psalm 26:8 (ESV): "O Lord, I love the habitation of your house, the place where your glory dwells." So what *is* the house of God? A lot of people may misunderstand what that means and for me, this distinction is a big passion point. The house of God, if I could express it and explain it and unpack it, is this: It's the presence of God, with the people of God, fulfilling the purpose of God.

You see that as we come together as God's people and we lift Him up, we praise and we sing and we worship Him. His presence comes, and that's a part of His purpose. We were created for Him, and we were created to worship Him. This is a part of our purpose, and it's holy ground.

This is where we become awakened to the presence of God. I looked up the word house in Hebrew: it means "receptacle" or "container." It's God's house—God's address—God's home. How many of you believe that there's no place like home? I love it when people come to our church for the first time. I'll engage with them: "Hey, what brought you here? What brought you back? What was it like? Tell me about your experience." I love it when they say, "Well, I walked into the building, and it just felt like *home.*"

You know what that says to me? That's the biggest compliment I could ever receive as a pastor because it tells me that God's presence, God's people, and God's purpose are in the house. You see? Everything you need is in the house.

This word receptacle stuck out to me. I began to think about this idea of an outlet—something else that's a receptacle. There are three holes in an outlet—if we draw the parallel with God's house, we're speaking about the Spirit—God's presence—as one, God's people as two, and God's purpose as three. There's power flowing to an outlet, but if I don't connect to it I can't receive the power from the house. See, if I get indifferent towards the house—if I get critical of the house—if I'm against the house, then I can't experience the power. We've paid for the power to pump into this outlet, but unless I plug into the receptacle I cannot benefit from the power.

And this is why you need to get plugged into God's house. I tell my church, "Hey, get connected to the local church," not because I'm some politician trying to get them behind an agenda, but because I'm a child of God and I'm in the house, and the secret to winning in life is being planted and plugged into God's house.

That's why the enemy fights to keep you out of God's house, to prevent you from staying there. Power flows from the house. Political power flows from the White House and the House of Representatives, but those houses do not even begin to compare with the power that flows from God's house.

I love the habitation.

So many times, we hear people say things like, "We're believing for a visitation," or, "God showed up, and it was powerful," or, "Lord, come, open the heavens and pour out your Spirit." But I want to catch us up on Acts 2. We don't have to pray prayers like that anymore. We don't have to pray, "God, pour out your Spirit." He's already poured everything He's going to pour. In Acts 2, the heavens were opened, and the Bible says they were never closed. So we don't have to pray for open heavens; we just have to get under the spout and drink what's already being poured out.

We don't have to pray for open heavens; we just have to get under the spout and drink what's already being poured out.

My prayer is that we would move from wanting a visitation to *believing for habitation*. In other words, "God, when You come, when we commune with You, we don't want You to leave. We want You to stay." When we operate like this wherever we go, the house of God is there. Where we go, the presence of God can be. It's not that God isn't in places; it's not that God is stronger over here. It's simply that His people, people of faith, understand how to enter in and receive—they become awakened to His presence.

I want to help you learn how to enter in—not just as a visitation, but as a habitation: a daily encounter where we dwell. Sometimes, it's a task for us to spend time with God. It can be challenging and inconvenient. We know we should do it, but we don't really want to do it. We simply do it because it's the right thing and we know that God likes it. However, it just hit me one day: do you realize that it is *never* hard for God to make room for you?

It is never a bother when you call on His name. I just pray that this truth helps us understand how much He loves us. When other people may not have time for you, there's an eternal, everlasting Father who's just waiting for you to invite Him, for you to commune with him. James 4:5

(NKJV) says, "The Spirit who dwells in us yearns jealously." For you. I want to walk in the habitation.

David was hungry for the habitation of the house. Hunger makes you desperate. I like to eat. I try to act like I don't, but I can't help it. You wouldn't like me when I'm hangry. When it comes to natural things, this is true, but what about a holy hunger? I want to stir our holy hunger. Think about it this way: Hunger is a sign of health. When someone gets sick or they have an ailment, they can lose their appetite. Holy hunger isn't about getting hangry—it's about getting desperate to live in the habitation of God's house, with His presence and His people, fulfilling His purpose.

Are you hungry?

The way that we satisfy our holy hunger in God's house is the habitation—the habit of worship. My prayer is that you get into the habit of daily worship—that the church isn't the only place that you worship but rather an amplification of your daily, personal worship. The house of God isn't just at one specific address—it's in every one of our homes.

People sometimes believe that they don't need the people of God to fulfill the purpose of God. They believe it can just be them and Jesus—that He's a personal, private Savior. But I'm telling you this: you cannot back that up biblically. You need people. You might be thinking, *I don't like people*. Well, I think we can each look in the mirror and point out a few things we don't like about ourselves. If we can learn to like ourselves despite those things, I think we can learn to enjoy and like people, too.

We need the presence and the people to fulfill purpose. It's individual worship *and* corporate worship.

Look at Hebrews 10:24-25 (ESV): "Let us consider how to stir one another to love and good works, not neglecting to meet together as is the habit of some. . . ." In other words, don't neglect this habit. It's the habit of worship individually and corporately, but it's also the habit of encouraging one other: "Encourage each other all the more as you see the Day is drawing nearer" (end of v. 25). His return is drawing nearer. It's so important that we catch a revelation of what it means to have the habitation in God's house and to be able to dwell there and let nothing keep us from the habit of worship, individually and corporately. I promise you, the enemy does not want that to happen—and that's why we've got to fight for it.

Turning Point Church has an incredible facility and an incredible worship team—a dream team that's ready to serve. Still, we have empty seats. I believe there's a day coming when we'll need to have overflow in the foyer because of the habitation of God's presence. When you understand the synergy of God's presence—that experience when two or more people worship together—we start to glimpse heaven. The Bible says that when we get to heaven it's going to be a sea of people and angels—an immeasurable number of people. Nations and tribes everywhere will come together, lifting up praise and singing, "Worthy is the Lamb, holy is the Lord forever" (Revelation 8:5-14, author paraphrase). Church is rehearsal for that time! That's why Sunday can be different than Wednesday. It's not because there are more people; it's that those people have a hunger for God's presence and are entering into it through worship and praise. There's a synergy.

I know one thing that God's put me on the planet to do is to help activate this intimate, passionate pursuit—to worship God and lead people to discover the power of His presence in the house of God.

Honor is important if you're going to understand the house of God. I love that the first letter of house is H. Honor. Remember when David said, "It's the place that your glory dwells" (Psalm 26:8, author paraphrase). The Hebrew word for glory means "weightiness," but it also means "wealth." It means "honor." So when I honor God in praise and worship, I attract His honor into my life. Worship starts with honor, and honor is humility in action. Pride will keep us from honor, but honor is the currency of elevation in the kingdom. Honor is the key to access in the kingdom. It starts with honor. Do you know what the key to honor is? Gratitude.

Worship starts with honor, and honor is humility in action.

Psalm 100:4 (author paraphrase) says, "Enter in his gates with thanksgiving. Go unto his courts with praise. Give praise and thanks to his name." So in praise and worship our goal—our heart—is to pour out gratitude. Gratefulness. When I become grateful, it births greatness in me. Gratitude gives birth to greatness. And there's greatness on the inside of you. When I give gratitude to God, it releases the greatness that's on the inside of me.

Ungratefulness causes dishonor. When I treat something as common, I dishonor it. So if honor attracts, dishonor repels. That's why, in relationships, when honor leaves a relationship it begins to go downhill. In friendship and in marriage, the Bible in Ephesians 5:21 is very clear that we should honor one another: "Submit to one another, take delight in honoring" (author paraphrase). Why? Because honor causes things to rise. Ungratefulness causes dishonor. When I am ungrateful, here's what happens: I lose my awe. I can't honor what I'm not grateful for.

You know how when you have a relationship, at first, everything is so exciting and new? You're talking on the phone—now, maybe it's texting—and sending emojis? Why do we do that? It's because we don't want to become familiar. We don't want to become ungrateful. Whatever we become ungrateful for, we begin to dishonor—and dishonor repels. So when I become ungrateful in the habitation of somebody that I'm really close to, I can take them for granted. It's amazing how a relationship that was so incredible to us at one point, because of ungratefulness and dishonor, can become a relationship in which we can no longer create the same feeling. It's not that *they* changed; it's that *we* changed.

We can become familiar in the habitation of relationship. Familiarity can dull us even from the presence of God. That's why someone can come into a church, their life a wreck, and cry out to God. God's presence in that place can change their life, and then something happens, and they get upset. All of a sudden, they walk into the same place and they cannot receive. They think God has left the building when really, God never left. If I'm willing and obedient, I'll eat the good of the land. See, willingness has to do with my attitude; obedience has to do with my action. That's why Jesus said, "If you remember that someone has something against you and you're at the alter worshiping and you remember this, leave your gift" (Matthew 5:23-24, author paraphrase), stop worshiping, stop singing, stop playing. Go make that thing right with the person and then come back and get your worship on.

We don't want to become familiar or ungrateful. We've got to get back. Jesus experienced familiarity in his hometown. Because they saw Him as the carpenter, they could not receive Him as the Christ. They were ungrateful for the gift of Christ in their lives. It doesn't mean that Jesus couldn't do miracles; it simply means that because of their ungratefulness, He wouldn't do it in their lives. See, gratitude is the key to honor, and honor is what gives us access.

We can't stop taking God's presence for granted in our daily lives. That's why we've got to stir one another in the house. We don't forsake the assembling together. Hopefully, when you come into church and I see you going after God, it stirs *me* up to go after God. When I see you smiling and serving and with your hands lifting and loving and hugging, it stirs me up. When I see you going after God, I'm like, *They're not going to get more than me, God. Let's get it on.* It's this stirring. Stir one another. That's why we've got to develop a heart of praise and thanksgiving—because worship is essential to the habitation of God's house. When you start your day, think, *This is the day that the Lord has made*. When you wake up in the morning, give thanks to God. When you enter the church, give thanks to God. Why? Because you enter in through gratitude.

Unless we perceive the greatness inside of us, we can never achieve it. God chose you. He created everything that there is for you. The sun sets for you. The forest—the leaves change for you. The church that Jesus is building . . . it's for you. That's why I have to learn to be grateful for everything. Commit to being in God's house and building God's house—because there are still sons and daughters out there who are far from God. When they do decide to show up, don't you think Father wants them to see us loving Him and loving each other—serving and giving and having joy in our lives? It all comes through worship. That's why we serve. That's why we pray. That's why we give of our finances.

Where there is no sacrifice, there is no worship. It costs you.

Finances are not about money; they're about worship. Finances represent your sweat, your skill, and your time. To give financially is a sacrifice. But here's the thing about worship: where there is no sacrifice, there is no worship. *It costs you*. Habitation costs you. It costs us to pray, to praise, to worship, to forgive, to serve, to love. That's why, at Turning Point, we have something called the legacy offering. It isn't just some veiled way to raise money. If it is, God help us. No: it's an invitation to worship God with your finances, so that you can honor God, give Him gratitude, give glory to God . . . and reach other sons and daughters in order to expand God's family. Worship requires sacrifice; where there is no sacrifice, there is no worship.

There was a time in David's life we read about in 2 Samuel 18-25 in which a plague was coming on the people of God. David decided he was going to worship God. He found a hill that he didn't own on which to make a sacrifice of worship. The farmer said to David, "Let me give you the wood and an animal to give the sacrifice. You're the king. I want to bless you. Come on, sir, let me bless you."

Look at what David said in 2 Samuel 24:24 (NLT): "But the king replied to [the farmer], 'No, I insist on buying it for I will not present burnt offerings to the LORD my God that have cost me nothing.'"

He would not offer the Lord anything that didn't cost him. Why? Because worship is sacrifice. And it's worth it!

That's why Jesus shed his blood for you. It cost Him because you were worth the sacrifice. God always honors sacrifice. I think about this practice of worshiping God and giving gratitude and dwelling in His presence, and I realize there's no other way I could have made it this far serving Jesus for the last twenty-six years. There's no way I could have made it in marriage twenty-three years, no way I could have made it as a parent twenty-one years. There's no way that I could celebrate 25 years of full-time vocational ministry and be healthy without God. I give the glory to God, but it isn't sustainable unless I love the habitation of His house—the place where His glory dwells.

Don't lose the awe and the wonder of God's house. Never view coming into a worship experience as something common. When you come in, be grateful. And when you can't see what God is doing, just remember what He's already done. Gratitude is the key to honor, and honor gives me access to His presence—and in His presence, everything changes.

Luke 7:36-50 tells the story of a woman who was a prostitute. Jesus was at a dinner, and she came into the room and broke open a costly fragrance. Theologians believe that this vial probably cost her life's savings. She opened it up and poured it on the Lord's feet; all the while she was weeping. There was a man at the dinner named Simon who looked at her and thought, *Why is He letting that prostitute touch him?*

Simon saw her as a despicable sinner—a piece of trash that needed to be discarded because he didn't see what Jesus saw. Even when people look at you and see certain things about you—what you've done, where you've been, what they've heard about you—remember that God doesn't see you that way.

Jesus, perceiving that Simon was having these thoughts, told a story about two people who owed someone a lot of money. One owed the man something like $100; the other owed a million. Jesus finished the story like this:

> *"So the owner of the money forgave both of their debts. Who do you think loved Him more? Who do you think was more appreciative?"*
> *"Oh," Simon answered, "the one that owed a million."*
> *Jesus said, "Yes, so it is. Who is forgiven much, loves much."*

He was saying, in essence, "She has sinned a lot, but man, look at her love now. Look at the sacrifice of her worship—look at her honor. Look at her gratitude." And by the way, all of us fall into the category of sinners. That's why we need to say yes to gratitude, to sacrificial worship.

The woman poured out the costly fragrance that used to attract men in the natural to her as a prostitute. But now she was redeeming it, pouring it on the man Christ Jesus. When she realized who He was and what He wanted to do, she redeemed her costly oil to worship the only One who really deserved it. Simon saw a sinful, worthless prostitute, but Jesus defended her. Jesus looked beyond her sinful past and saw her as a worshiper. He saw her as forgiven. He saw her in forgiveness, in honor. He saw her restored.

This is the beauty of what can happen in God's house when we come in with gratitude, humble ourselves, and honor the great King. It doesn't matter where we've been. In fact, Jesus never even had to say the words, "You're forgiven," when she began to worship and give gratitude. Jesus forgave her, redeemed her, and brought His life into hers. She was forever changed after encountering Him and worshiping at His feet.

Your sins are forgiven, and God will give you beauty for ashes. He'll turn your mourning into dancing, your mistakes into miracles. When's the last time you found yourself weeping in worship at the feet of Jesus? Just think about that. There's no condemnation in Christ, but my prayer is that we would get to a place of gratitude. When I began to reflect in a moment of worship on where God has brought me from—what I should have gotten, what I deserved—and the dignity and honor that He restored to me . . . that he would honor me and my family . . . who am I? It brings me to my knees. It brings me to tears. See, that's what worship is, it's remembering who He is and what He's done, and it's also remembering what He says we are. God sees what you don't see. My prayer is that you would see what He sees.

When's the last time you found yourself weeping in worship at the feet of Jesus?

The woman came before Jesus with something that cost her. We worship because we're grateful. I don't know what you've been facing. I don't know what you've been dwelling on. But maybe the enemy or other people have tried to make you feel like trash, like you're a failure, that you don't matter. Jesus sees you not in your past, but in your future: You are cleansed. You are whole. You are blessed. You are chosen. You are a royal expression of His grace and of His majesty. You are free.

Let's plug into the power. Let's plug into His presence. Begin to give thanks to Him right now. In His presence, depression has to go. Anxiety has to leave. Fear dies, demons tremble, and victory is obtained. Joy springs forth. If you're ready for God to do something He's never done, you've got to do something you've never done. Go after God's presence. Walk in the habitation!

SECTION TWO

THE PEOPLE OF GOD

CHAPTER 5
WE > ME

I f the vision—the systems and structures—is the seed, then culture is the soil of the house. When the soil is good, the seed will grow.

You can take a system from another organization and try to make it work in your church, but if your soil is no good, that seed won't work. You can have excellent seed, but it won't grow. The most fertile layer of soil is humus. That word stems from humility. This is why it takes humility to have a fertile culture. We've got to be teachable. If I'm proud,

I get upset when people try to correct me. The Bible says that we are to be clothed in humility. Remember, humility is the key to honor.

The culture of our homes and churches is important. You can have a great mission statement and profile picture on Instagram, but if the culture of your marriage stinks, it won't be good. Make sure that you're tending to the culture of your home, your relationships, and your team. Whatever we turn a blind eye to will eventually become a blind spot.

We believe that the soil of a healthy church is made up of honor, ownership, unity, servant leadership, and excellence. As we do our best to live that out, we're discipling others. What happens then is that those individuals take those qualities back to their homes, teams, and school. This isn't about dictatorship. This is about discipleship, about a family guarding the culture of God's house. When you're planted in the soil, your life should change—it should flourish. There should be good things growing out of your life.

The next element of the house of God is the people of God—the family of God. Sunday is God's idea. And it's His eternal desire for every person to call upon His name. Psalm 68:6 (NLT) says, "God places the lonely and families, and he sets the prisoners free, and gives them joy."

Think about this: God's answer to loneliness is family. Were you ever in a game in school in which team captains were picking teammates? Have you ever been the last person picked for something? The feeling isn't great, is it? You don't feel valued. The worst is when you don't get picked at all because there was an uneven number of people. It's a terrible experience. But here's the truth: You did not choose Christ. He chose you. Jesus tells us that God decided to bring you to Himself through Christ. He chose you beforehand! So don't let anybody ever tell you that you don't matter, that you don't have value, that you're damaged goods, or that you're a mistake. In Christ, the Word tells us that we are chosen—part of God's family. You're a part of a family by choice.

Jesus is building His church, and He wants every one of His children to be a part of a local life-giving church. He wants us in community. One of the passions of my heart is bringing people to a place of believing that. Can you imagine if every Christian believed that they belonged to a local life-giving church and was committed for life to it? That's a biblical expectation! We've got to help people value and honor the local church. It truly is the greatest thing on planet Earth. It's not the easiest thing, but it's what Jesus is building. It's what Jesus is coming back for. It's what Jesus is about, and He created us for community. But in order for us to have community, we've got to come into unity.

Community is like a decree—when we come with brothers and sisters before God. Ephesians 2:18-19 (NIV) tells us, "For through him we both have access to the Father by one Spirit. Consequently, you are no longer foreigners and strangers, but fellow citizens with God's people and also members of his household." Here's the key: You belong in God's family. Psalm 122:1 (NLT) says, "I was glad when they said to me, 'Let us go to the house of the LORD.'" That's one thing we've always believed would be the mindset of our family at Turning Point—that everybody would be excited when it's Sunday.

Maybe you grew up in a church where you were sad when they said, "Let's go to the house." Or maybe you were mad. But I believe we should be glad. It's the people of God. There is no us without Him. I've served now in full-time ministry for twenty-five years, and I've followed Jesus for twenty-seven years. I have found this to be true: people believe that they can truly love Christ but not His people. I believe that Christ is the head, and His people are the body. It's a package deal. If you want to love Jesus, you have to take His people.

If you want to love Jesus, you have to take His people.

Many people today live in a dead zone, and they're stuck because they believe they don't have to be connected to a local church, a local vision. In their mind, they know Jesus personally, and it doesn't matter if they get connected. This is a stronghold that's hindering the body of Christ from fulfilling its mission in the earth. It's a way of thinking that keeps people from a way of doing. They're not experiencing God's best. You can never flourish unless you embrace not only the presence of God but also the people of God.

I've had enough of pastors getting on Instagram and doing these little videos where they say they're so grieved by the body of Christ. I'm just tired of hearing it. I'm like, "What church do you go to?" For some reason, it's almost cool to come down on churches, but the lives of those in our church have been changed. They like it better than Disney World. They're on fire. But for some reason, we feel like we have to cut down the body of Christ to other pastors in order to make ourselves look good. Any time you have to cut somebody else down, you're elevating yourself, which again, goes against the principle of humility that's so important to a healthy culture. It's self-righteousness.

I want to make sure in our culture that we're for the "big C" church. We don't cut down churches or pastors—all that does is hurt the body, the witness. How many people leave a church and, instead of taking personal responsibility for the way they handled themselves, point and sling mud on that church? As a family of choice, we've got to make sure that we understand the power of loving God's church. Any time you cover and love God's church, Jesus is for that. It's not that there's no accountability, correction, or rebuke. Jesus rebuked seven churches in the book of Revelation. But only Jesus has the right to do that. He gave us the way to restoration and repentance.

She's not perfect, but there is a bride that is making herself ready. Revelation 22:17 (author paraphrase) says, "Let the bride and the Spirit say, 'Come, Lord Jesus.'" Let's make sure we're doing everything we can to be our best for God—to represent Christ in the body, and to build up the body of Christ. Isn't that what the Word tells us—to build each other up, encourage one another, pray for one another, serve one another, love the church? In fact, that's what Jesus said when He was talking privately with Peter after his betrayal and Christ's resurrection: "If you love me, Peter, . . ." Did He say, "Beat up my church. Rebuke my church. Cut it down. Point out its faults"? No. He said, "Feed my sheep.

Feed my lambs." I implore you, elders: Shepherd the flock of God which is among you. Don't do it out of compulsion. Don't do it for selfish gain. Don't do it for a paycheck. Do it because you love the Lord.

You can't be in fellowship with the groom and not the bride. My wife and I are one. And if you're going to be in fellowship and alignment with us, you can't just like me and not like her. We're one together. It's the same way with God's people and the local church. One of the things the enemy tries to do is slander God by misquoting the Word to you. He'll point out partial truth and try to make you believe it. He asked Adam and Eve, "Did God really say?" One of the half-truths he peddles to Christians is that you don't have to go to church to go to heaven.

Think about that statement. Is that true? It's not a heaven or hell issue. But if you're truly going to heaven, why wouldn't you want to be in church? When I got saved, no one had to motivate me to go to church. You couldn't keep me out of it. Every time the doors were open, I was there. The Holy Spirit internally motivates us to realize, *I need to be a part of the body. I need to be in the place of God. I need to be in the presence of God, with the people of God, fulfilling the purpose of God.*

We're better together, stronger together, and smarter together. We sometimes separate Jesus from His people. I tell people often, "If you follow Christ but don't like people, you won't enjoy heaven." If the devil can keep us from the people of God, he can keep us from the promises of God. Individualism is one of the greatest deceptions the enemy uses to lure people away from the place they were created to be: in the body of Christ in Christ-centered community.

> If the devil can keep us from the people of God,
> he can keep us from the promises of God.

John 3:16 (NIV) says, "For God so loved the world that he gave his only son that whoever believes in him wouldn't perish, but have everlasting life." God loves people. God loves His church. The cross is vertical and horizontal: it suspended Jesus, the Christ, between heaven and earth. Not only was the cross of Christ reconciling us to God vertically—it was also reconciling us horizontally. In fact, that's why we are reconcilers. We have the message of reconciliation. Jesus broke down the wall of hostility so that there could be unity. Think about it: He was pierced in His side, and the Bible says that water and blood flowed. Isn't it interesting that the second Adam was pierced in His side near His rib just like the first Adam when God created Eve out of Adam's rib?

Jesus being pierced in His side was a birthing of the bride of Christ, the church, which we see in Acts 2. We are the bride. We are living stones. We are the temple. We are the body. We are the house of God.

The *Great Calling* is to be fruitful and multiply. The *Great Commandment* is to love your neighbor as yourself. And the *Great Commission* (in Matthew 28), is to carry this news into all the world. Isn't it interesting that all three are about people?

"Go, be fruitful." Multiply what? People.

"Go, love me, and love people."

"Go into all the world, preach the good news, baptize—transmit a way of thinking."

It's all about people.

Jesus is a personal Savior but not an exclusive parent. You're not an only child. I was in a health club one time witnessing to a guy with whom I'd struck up a bit of a rapport. I said, "Hey, are you a believer?"

He was like, "Yeah."

I said, "That's awesome. And how's your walk with Jesus going?"

He got really mad at me, and he said, "That is a very private thing. That's a private conversation. I don't have to tell you anything."

I said, "Oh, excuse me."

Yes, Jesus is a personal Savior, but our faith in Him is not private. It's not an exclusive talk between you and Jesus—we are children. We are family. Romans 8:29 (NLT) says this: "For God knew his people in advance and he chose them to become like his son so that his son would be the firstborn among many brothers and sisters." So again, we see that Jesus knew His people. He chose them. And He is the firstborn among many brothers and sisters.

Psalm 133 (NLT) describes how we ought to live as such:

> *How wonderful and pleasant it is*
> *when brothers live together in harmony!*
> *For harmony is as precious as the anointing oil*
> *that was poured over Aaron's head,*
> *that ran down his beard*
> *and onto the border of his robe.*
> *Harmony is as refreshing as the dew from Mount Hermon*
> *that falls on the mountains of Zion.*
> *And there the LORD has pronounced his blessing,*
> *even life everlasting.*

This is why when we come together and live in unity God commands the blessing. It's there that the anointing flows. It's there that God releases life. No wonder the enemy wants to keep us apart and divided—he wants to stop the anointing and the blessing of God from flowing to us and on us and through us.

When we live in unity, God commands the blessing, the anointing flows, and God releases life.

Ephesians 4 tells us that the gifts of the apostles, the prophets, the evangelists, the pastors, and the teachers are to equip us to do the work of ministry so that we will mature and grow up in Christ. God wants us to mature because the enemy keeps on dividing us. Whether it's as Democrats, Republicans, black, white, brown, yellow, conservatives, liberals, masks, no masks, vax, no vax—the enemy loves to keep us divided because it keeps us from unity which is really about the glory and the anointing flowing. We have to be willing to live in the middle like Jesus did. He was a bridge. We've got to lay down our lives and be willing to stretch and even to be walked over. We've got to give up our right to be right because the goal is unity. I'm not talking about the world. I'm talking about the body—the family of God. This way, the oil and the blessing can flow and impact the world, so they can see Jesus.

The Bible says that they will know that we are His true disciples by our love for one another. I like to say it like this: "Let me show you my love for God by how well I love and honor you." Remember how Psalm 133 talked about the dew on Mount Hermon? Mount Hermon is a nine thousand-foot peak, and it gets snow caps. The dew will come off of that snow cap and fall onto the mountains of Zion. By the time you get to the foot of Mount Zion, there's a spring, and these springs go off into little streams, until eventually, they all fill the Jordan River. You can actually kayak down the rapids of the Jordan. So, think about it: It starts small at the top, with tiny drops of dew. But by the time all these drops come together into a stream, they end up a rushing stream. That's why together we're better. That's why "we" is greater than "me."

I'm not afraid of a little raindrop, but you get me in some rapids, and I'm white-knuckling it. Unity brings momentum into my life!

If we can get people moving together in the same direction, we're a powerful force in the earth. How difficult it can be just to get people to buy into the vision of the church! That's our greatest challenge: keeping our teams united and focused, moving together in the same direction without becoming offended and bitter and hurting each other and hating each other and quitting. It's important that we understand the power of culture, discipleship, and leadership.

When we partner with God and His people, His presence and power begin to flow in us and through us. They begin to push us as well as those around us forward and higher. God wants us to get rolling forward with force, to grow with intensity and strength. He doesn't want us to make commitments in a moment, in passion, only to see those commitments fizzle out a few days later. God wants us free from frustrated Christianity, where we get pumped up and ready to charge hell with a water pistol only to stall out in the wilderness, depressed and discouraged.

Israel left Egypt with signs and wonders. They left with the wealth of Egypt, but they stalled out in the desert, and what should've taken two weeks took forty years. Then there was the early church: Jesus ascended to heaven, the Holy Spirit came and filled 120 disciples, and they were united. The Bible says they were in one accord. They were in unity. They were praying. They were moving in the same direction. The Word of

God was preached, and when the church was birthed, five thousand were added. They were rolling stones.

You know, snowflakes aren't intimidating by themselves, but if you get enough snowflakes moving in the same direction, they become an avalanche—and that's very intimidating. That's why we've got to understand that we're living in a time in which Jesus is building His church, and the church is growing stronger. I don't care what you see on Facebook. I don't care what you see on Instagram. The church, not just in America, but around the world, is growing by the millions. There is revival in China, in the Middle East, in South America, and Africa. It is actually America that has the smallest churches in the world.

Korea had a church of a million. There are churches in Africa that have a million seats in them. The media and the world and America want you to think that the church is going to hell in a handbasket. I'm telling you that Jesus is building His church around the world. That's why we've got to fight in our generation to make sure that the church is strong and growing and thriving. If we don't embrace what I'm talking about today, America will become like the relic that Europe is—there were great movements, great apostles, great revivals, but now?

God is setting up America for revival. He's mobilizing His church in preparation for His return. We want to get into the flow of His presence with His people. So we don't want to just manage momentum; we want to make the most of it. Momentum is determined by how much and how fast something is moving in the same direction. Physics says that the lower to the ground an object is, the faster it can go. That's why we want to stay humble in God's presence and with God's people. We can't shrink back, but we've got to roll on. Don't fall away.

So the enemy's trying to keep us divided. What's the solution? What can we do? What's our counterattack? It's to get closer to Jesus and to each other. We can't allow space. In marriage, in family, and even in our teams, if there is tension, it has to be addressed. Don't dismiss things that you know you need to address in a relationship—as difficult as it may be. If you don't deal with it, it will eventually deal with you. Let's love our relationships enough to stay closer together. And if you're misunderstood, if you're offended, if you're upset, if you're angry, make sure that you make peace, that you talk, that you get closer to Jesus and one another. Let's make sure that we're growing closer to Jesus and staying close to each other.

Ron Carpenter told me this: "Things that you don't speak to die. Things that you speak to live." John Gordon puts it this way: "When there is no communication, it automatically fills up with negativity."[4] Think about that. When you don't talk to your teen, your spouse, your friends, or your leaders, the default for that space is negativity. What happens is that the enemy sees that there's no communication and starts building this narrative of what they think about you: They don't care about you. They have hidden motives. All of a sudden, the enemy's gotten into your ear and built a believable case for something that's not even true.

---

4 John Gordon, "Where There Is a Void Negativity Will Fill It," *Jon Gordon*, 24 Oct. 2016, http://www.jongordon.com/positive-tip-void.html.

We need to have the hard conversations—to address the issues. When you feel like something's going on, be honest about it. Why? Because we value the relationships and don't want them to be hindered. We've got to be clothed with humility. We're going to talk about conflict resolution, freedom from offense, and embracing hard conversations. We're going to talk about the F word: forgiveness. I really believe that, if we can get people united, we're going to be an unstoppable force in the earth. There won't be high turnover in churches because there will be health and relationship and kingdom unity. Are you with me?

When we get closer together, we're going to get tighter—we will literally start holding each other up. Have you seen the redwood forests? These trees are 350 feet tall. Here's the miracle of the redwoods: they're the oldest living organisms on planet Earth, but their roots are only five feet deep. And they're really close to each other. You know why they live so long? It's because their roots are entwined, and they're so close together. If a storm comes, they lean on each other. That's a beautiful picture of what the people of God should be doing—extending our love, extending our branches, being planted in the house. We're together, holding each other up, growing together. We're fruitful, and we're flourishing.

Paul wrote this in Romans 1:11-12 (NLT):

For I long to visit you so I can bring you some spiritual gift that will help you grow strong in the LORD. When we get together, I want to encourage you in your faith, but I also want to be encouraged by yours.

We need each other to maximize our potential. It's critical that we come together consistently and cling to each other. If I take twenty-four hours off with prayerlessness—no Word, no faith, no worship—if I'm not daily encountering Jesus and connecting with others who do, I can lose my fire.

There's a story about a man who had been faithfully attending church for years but no longer thought he needed to come anymore. He decided to just relax on Sunday. The pastor lovingly went to his house one night in the winter. He was sitting by the fire when the pastor came in. The pastor didn't say anything for about thirty minutes—he simply sat with him, watching the fire pop. Then, the pastor got up and took the tongs to grab a coal from the hottest part of the fire. He pulled it out and set it on the end of the brick hearth and sat back down in his chair. They kept staring at the fire. At first, that ember was glowing. It would burn you. But after about twenty minutes, it became smoking ash. The pastor simply got up and walked out.

The next Sunday, guess what? That man was back in church. He understood the message. No matter how hot I may feel today, eventually, if I'm not in the fire, I'm going to fizzle out. That's why it's so important for us to love the gathering. That's why it's so important for us to lead people to the gathering. That's why it's so important for us to be passionate about the gathering—because we maximize our momentum and spur one another on to love and good deeds when we come together. It's like a fire in a fireplace.

That's why, on Sunday, we say, "Get out there and talk to people." Encourage your team. Send them thank you cards. Why? Because you're stoking that fire. People are out in workplaces, in the world. We've got to lead them into small group, teen night, breakfasts and coffees, and places in which we can do life with them. They don't get that out there. As pastors and ministers, we're always around it; our temptation is simply to do life here—we're not available Friday and Saturday. But we're never going to see a growing, thriving church when we think like that. Let's make sure that we stoke the fire.

"Let us consider," Hebrews 10:24-25 (ESV) tells us, "how to stir up one another to love and good works, not neglecting to meet together as is the habit of some, but encouraging one another all the more as you see the day approaching." If you see somebody who wasn't at church on Sunday, make sure you're reaching out to them. All it takes is one or two weeks. COVID has proven that. People were out of church for nine weeks—some have never come back. Thirty-three percent said they're never coming back. They just need to get on fire!

> When we are united as the family of God, a family of choice, we will shine with the glory of God to those people who sit in darkness.

Romans 15:1 (author paraphrase) says, "We who have strong faith should help those who are weak." In your strengths, reach out and help others become strong. Stir them up. Motivate them. Encourage them. That's why we're the body of Christ. When one part of the body suffers, it affects the whole body. When someone's not fulfilling their function, it impacts the whole body. God wants us blazing with His life and His Spirit. That's why coming consistently is so important. That's why we live the weekly gathering. We talk about it. We hear it out. Because we believe that when we come together daily and weekly—especially all the more as we see the day approaching—when we are united as the family of God, a family of choice, we will shine with the glory of God to those people who sit in darkness so that they can see Christ—the way, the truth, and the life—the path of forgiveness, freedom and healing, and purpose. They, too, can move from loneliness and find their place in the family of God.

CHAPTER 6

RIGHT ALIGNMENTS FOR RIGHT ASSIGNMENTS

f we are to flourish like a palm tree or grow like a cedar, then we have to be planted in the house of God. In order for a tree to be fruitful, it has to be planted. The better the soil, the better the results. According to the Word of God, we are fruitful because we are planted.

What are we planted in? What is the soil? I believe it's found in Christ and in His church. The local church is a part of the house of God, and it is the soil in which God is able to get us rooted, nurtured, and grown, so we can fulfill our God-given potential and purpose.

The local church is God's plan to reach, pastor, disciple, and mobilize His people in the earth. Yes, we abide in the presence—yes, He is the vine—but His house, His church, is the soil. Jesus said, "I tell you the truth, unless a kernel of wheat is planted in the soil and dies, it remains alone. But its death will produce many new kernels—a plentiful harvest of new lives" (John 12:24, NLT).

If we want to be fruitful and multiply, we have to be willing to die to our self-will and selfishness to have meaningful, purpose-driven relationships in the kingdom of God. Whether it be our relationship with God, our parents, our siblings, our spouses, our friends, or, yes, the family of God, we must deny ourselves in the soil of relationship, so we can become the best version of ourselves. It's how we grow best: within the context of close Christ-centered relationships.

We can apply this to all of our relationships. For instance, my wife, Charla, and me: if we want our relationship to bear fruit and impact other lives—our children, our family, our friends, the family of God— we have to deny ourselves daily and serve one another, honor and love another even when we don't *feel* like it. We have to learn to "faith our way into a feeling" instead of feeling our way into an action. If I want to stop the good results that God can bring forth out of my marriage, all I need to do is think that it's all about me and what I want—my needs: "I am the X factor in my relationship." Conversely, the best gift I can give to my relationships is a healthy version of myself that has submitted to the lordship of Jesus. I must take on the mindset of a servant to Christ in every relationship in my life.

I want to focus on this truth when it comes to the house of God—the local church—our family of choice. You see, the *people of God* is the second element of the house of God, and this is where I've seen so many people become hurt, wounded, and offended, and go on to cause even more damage to the work of Christ in the earth. My heart and my prayer is that this teaching can help us all learn how to surrender to Christ even more, and take on the form of a humble servant filled with God's unconditional love and grace, stepping into love like Jesus did.

I often teach others that, when we enter into a relationship, we put unspoken, unrealistic expectations on others. When we don't communicate these expectations and they aren't met, we become disappointed. That disappointment can lead to ungratefulness that eventually leads to dishonor. When honor leaves any relationship, so does the quality of that relationship. I realized this when I got married to my wife, Charla. I had unspoken expectations towards her that I didn't even recognize. When I was growing up, on Saturday mornings, my mother would get up early and clean the house and cook me breakfast before I watched cartoons. I would wake up to the sound of a vacuum cleaner, the house smelling like Pledge furniture cleaner, bacon, pancakes, grits, toast and jelly, and chocolate milk. Yes, I love breakfast, and I like to eat. That was the norm for me every Saturday growing up.

When I got married to my wife, I never expressed that, but I found myself early on in the first year of our marriage waking up on Saturday and being somewhat frustrated and irritated. I didn't really know why. Now, on Saturday mornings at my wife's house growing up, they slept in until 10:30 or 11:00 a.m. They didn't get up early and start cleaning or cooking. So I would wake up on a Saturday morning with an expectation, and my wife was in bed sleeping really well. My unrealized expectation created strife in our relationship. Once I was able to identify it through my time with the Lord—submitting myself to Him—He showed me this. I died to myself and my expectation. We had a conversation about it, laughed about it, and I never put that expectation on her anymore. I put the expectation back on myself.

In fact, as I was writing this book, my father was admitted to the hospital in February of 2022, where he was diagnosed with terminal cancer and given only six months to live. This was just three months after his Thanksgiving visit with us. I asked my father if he were willing to come to my home, and he agreed.

My wife and children were so gracious, compassionate, and caring towards him. I was able to care for my father by helping him out of his bed, getting him into his wheelchair, and wheeling him around outside for fresh air. I was able to feed him, give him drink, and make him comfortable. We were able to pray and sing over him and surround him with so much love. We had no idea he would only be with us for four days before going to heaven.

It was my great honor to be there for my dad, to hug him and kiss his head, telling him I loved him. I was overwhelmed with emotion thinking of how God was still allowing places in my heart to be healed that I didn't even know needed it. I felt as if all the years of not having my father's affection were compounded into those four days caring for him in our home. God restored the years the enemy had stolen because, by His grace, I was willing to be open to serving my father as Christ has served me with unconditional love.

If we're going to flourish in life—in relationships—in the house of God—we've got to take the expectations off of others and put them back on ourselves. Many times, we can expect something of others that we don't even expect of ourselves. This is just one aspect of what I mean when I talk about dying to and denying yourself. Once I denied myself, it was never an issue again. In fact, my wife will try to get up and cook me breakfast on Saturdays when she can. But if she can't, I cook it myself—or I might even sleep in with her. So many times, we exalt an issue over our relationships—and that's what hinders us from flourishing in those relationships.

As a church, we pray, we serve, and we give to reach new families—and it's our joy, our calling to do so. However, way too often, families come in and encounter the presence of God, they are encouraged and loved by the people of God, and they start fulfilling the purpose of God—but because they were not aware of the *expectations* that they have put on others, they become disappointed and ungrateful. This leads to dishonor, and they end up leaving the very place where God changed their lives.

I am by no means excusing wrong behavior, bad leadership, or unhealthy relationships. Please hear my heart on that; however, at the same time, if we never come to the table as Jesus tells us in Matthew 18—if we never go to people and make an effort to restore the relationship—we'll never move forward in the purpose God has for that relationship. Our default is to not address the issue; instead, we tend to abandon or abort the relationship and its purpose. I can give you an example of how I saw this play out in my own life.

As a child, I was my mother and father's only child—not by choice but because they couldn't have any more children after me. By the time I was five, they were divorced. My father left because things didn't work out between them. I don't know what expectations they may have placed upon each other. With all due respect, they didn't have anybody modeling it for them. They certainly didn't have a mentor or a pastor in their lives coaching them or helping them to learn how to resolve conflict. My father went on to remarry, as did my mother many years later, but as a teenager and a young twenty-something, it was very difficult growing up without a father.

I had a lot of anger towards my dad. I never had a conversation with him, but I had an expectation of him—and rightly so, as his son. The problem was that I never gave him the chance to repent and reconcile in the relationship. If you've been through divorce, as a child or an adult, I recommend my book, *Watch Me Daddy*, where you can read the full story of my experience with my father and being raised by a single mom.

I began to follow and surrender to Christ, and I got planted in the soil of the local church. I moved under the leadership of a godly pastor who became a spiritual father in my life. That's when healing began to happen. What I learned was that, in one relationship with my biological father, I was wounded, but God brought healing to my life through a spiritual father. This is a very powerful principle when it comes to the people of God. Many times, we have been hurt deeply by people, and our default is to stay away from people —that's why we won't get into the soil of the local church. We won't become committed to a body of believers. We certainly won't submit to crisis leadership in our lives through a pastor, leader, or spiritual mother or father. We're afraid because we have been hurt by people.

You can never fulfill your purpose or potential apart from people.

The enemy begins to make us believe that we can't get close to people because people hurt us. But I'm here to tell you that you can never fulfill your purpose or potential apart from people. And yes, people hurt us, but it's also through people that God heals us. Simply said, people hurt us, but people heal us, so we don't want to avoid community. We don't want to avoid the people of God in an effort to protect ourselves—that doesn't work in relationships. We have to humble ourselves before God, surrender to Christ, take on the form of a servant, be filled with His grace, and get planted in a local church under its leadership so that we can grow and bring forth good things so that we can see reconciliation and healing happen.

As Jesus said, many new lives will be impacted because of the healing that happens in our lives. What the devil meant for evil God turns around for good—just like the story of Joseph and his brothers. As I humbled myself to Christ's lordship, as I got planted in the soil of a local, life-giving church under a good pastor—not a perfect pastor, but a good pastor who loved God, loved his wife, loved his family, and loved me—I was able to see my father in a different light. I was able to realize that he didn't grow up with a great dad; my father was battling depression and out of work. As God began to help me to see him through His eyes, my heart was moved with compassion.

I was able to approach my father with a Bible that I had his name engraved on, a coconut cake, and a set of cassette tapes of teaching and preaching that had impacted my life. As I went to my father with these gifts, as I talked about my expectations and expressed them, I was able to hear his heart. He didn't even realize some of the things I told him because I'd never given him the opportunity to hear them. After that conversation, he was able to repent and say, "I'm sorry. Will you forgive me?" Our relationship was healed. My dad came out of depression, gave his life to Christ, asked me to baptize him, became a part of our church, and began to read his Bible, and God was able to bring restoration that is still happening today.

In fact, this past Thanksgiving, I drove down to Florida to pick my dad up—he had Thanksgiving with me and my family for the first time ever. He watched me preach in the church we planted nineteen years ago. My dad and I are closer than ever, and he's also closer with his grandchildren and my wife. My point in sharing this isn't to brag—my point is that we have to deny ourselves and our rights. We have to give up our right to be right, our right to be offended. We have to lay down our pride and risk the vulnerability that comes with restoration. The truth is that my dad could have said, "I didn't do anything wrong. Get out of here, kid! You're on your own." That could have happened, but it didn't. Because I was willing to risk that, the Holy Spirit was able to work, and restoration happened.

If we're going to flourish in the house of God, if we're going to flourish in relationships, we have to deny ourselves, surrender to Christ, put the expectation back on us, and believe that through Christ we can do all things. I am the greatest factor of seeing healing and restoration happen in any relationship that I am in—and that includes the local church I choose to join.

If I am the seed, as Jesus said, I must die to myself and get under the soil. Again, the soil of the house of God is the presence of God in the people of God who are committed to fulfilling the purpose of God. God wants us to be under His authority, but also His delegated authority—the leadership of the local church. Many people don't understand authority—and they certainly don't honor it! We can see that every day in our nation. But the Bible teaches that God is all about honor.

The only commandment of the Ten Commandments that has a promise connected to it is the one regarding honoring our fathers and mothers:

the authorities that God gives to us in life. And yes, I know firsthand what it's like to have a father that I didn't feel deserved honor because of his actions—because of his absence. However, God still commanded me to honor him. Honor is given not when it's deserved but because we honor God. I'm able to honor others because I see them as precious to God. That's extremely difficult, but when we look to God, His grace and His spirit will empower us to be people of honor. I wholeheartedly believe the Bible is clear that we are to honor God's authority in every way, including His delegated authority in the local church.

Honor is the first lesson God wants us to learn as His sons and daughters. Honor means we place proper weight and value upon some thing or someone. As we said before, honor attracts blessing into our lives, while dishonor attracts negative things—or what the Bible calls "cursing"— into our lives. Honor gives me access. Whatever honor I inherit will take me further in life: in education, skill, charisma, and the like.

I believe God has called us to bring honor back to the house of God, our families, our marriages, our communities, and our world by being honorable people. That's why Romans 12:10 (NLT) says, "Take delight in honoring one another." Scripture also teaches that humility precedes honor, so if we're going to be honorable, we have to deny ourselves and humble ourselves into the soil God's house. When we do, we will burst forth abundant fruit that remains to the glory of the Father.

To drive this point further home, let's look at the story of a centurion that came to Jesus because He wanted his servant to be healed. In Matthew 8:7-8 (author paraphrase), Jesus said, "I will come and heal him," but the centurion said, "I'm not worthy to have you come to my house—just send your word and it will happen." The centurion said, "I'm a man under authority. I do what my commander says, and I have soldiers under me who carry out my authority, so I understand that, if you just speak the word, it will happen."

Jesus marveled at this man's faith. Because the centurion was under authority, it empowered him to *have* authority. I believe God wants us to get under the things He wants us to get under so that He can put us over the things He wants us to be over. And in order to walk in true kingdom authority, we need to be *under* kingdom authority.

In order to walk in true kingdom authority, we need to be under kingdom authority.

It goes without saying that this is not easy—especially if you're under an unhealthy leader. There are unhealthy leaders who misuse and abuse the authority God has given to them. This does not make it right at any level. Whether it's a leader in a church, a home, a business, or a government, Jesus taught us that, as believers, we don't operate in authority as the world does: lording it over people. In the kingdom, we use our authority to serve people, not for selfish ambition and gain. We use our authority because we love the Father and want to serve our family of choice.

I understand that, as a husband, I have authority over my wife, but I don't use that authority to rule her and dominate her, but instead to serve, steward, pastor, love, cherish, and protect her. The same is true with my children. My authority isn't given to me so that I can control, abuse, and manipulate them but so that I can father them, bless, equip, correct, encourage and train them up in the way that they should go.

The same as true as a pastor and a spiritual father. God has entrusted me with His authority, His anointing, but as a steward who is accountable to Him for how I use that authority. No, I'm not perfect, and yes, I need grace. I've learned—and I'm still learning—how to get better and to never misuse my authority because of my love and reverence for the One who gave it to me. This is a lesson I had to learn the hard way because of my relationship with my father—or lack thereof. I did not like authority, nor did I trust it or follow it—which is probably why I had confrontations with my teachers, principals, coaches, and even bosses before I surrendered to the authority of Christ.

This attitude attracted every negative thing and curse into my life, but there came a point where the authority I was confronting had the power to put me in handcuffs and in jail overnight, which is the place you go when you cannot honor authority. They take away your freedom and put you in a cell. But thank God, He led me to a local church with a loving pastor who became a spiritual father who believed in me, encouraged me and, yes, even rebuked me. But I knew he loved me, and I could receive it. It was there that I realized God had put authority in my life not to keep me down, oppress me, or use me but to develop me, equip me, and grow me to go to places I never would have gotten to without that authority.

I have learned to honor, respect, and value authority in my life. In fact, today, even as a senior pastor and founder of a local church, I still have men in my life whom I am under—not by force but by choice. I believe we should all be under godly, loving leadership if we truly want to flourish in life and in the house of God. I would not be where I am today if I hadn't learned the lesson of honor. That's why I'm so passionate about helping others understand it—so that they, too, can experience the reward.

It's going to be hard. But we get to choose our hard. Having a good marriage is hard and going through divorce is hard. Having a good family is hard and having a bad family is hard. Being a part of a local, life-giving church is hard and not being a part of a local, life-giving church is hard. Choose your hard.

RIGHT ALIGNMENTS LEAD TO RIGHT ASSIGNMENTS

When I finally decided to commit to being a part of church and learning about the Bible, I started Bible college. It wasn't because I felt called to be a pastor, but I wanted to understand Sunday's message. Once I decided to grow in that, and I began to serve, I began to feel that value, that dignity. Eventually, I was invited to be the singles Sunday school teacher.

Somehow, I went from Sunday school teacher to pastor. That summer we had a worship leader who had a lot of charisma, humor, and wit.

We really bonded. He saw things in me I didn't see in myself. He'd tell me things like, "You just have no clue the magnitude of the calling on your life, do you?"

I'm like, "I don't know what you're talking about, dude." But I began to believe. This worship leader had opportunities to be a part of another large church in Orlando, and I had an opportunity to go with him. It was a megachurch of around three thousand at the time. They had a TV ministry, and the pastor of the church was well-known.

I loved worship—I thought that this was God's moment for me: a kind of "Elijah" calling. I'd learn, go to this church, and get this opportunity, this platform. However, both my pastor at the time and the worship leader told me, "We don't think this is God. But we'll bless and release you." They loved me enough to tell me the truth. And that freed me up to make decisions. It's like the prodigal father letting go of his son.

Even in my own life as a father, I go back to the prodigal father. When his son came to him and said, "Dad, I want my inheritance—you're not dying quick enough—give me my money now," the dad was in his old age. The young man was probably between nineteen to twenty-five. As a young adult in Jewish culture, you're supposed to stick around and take care of your parents—honor your father and mother. But the father didn't counsel him. The father didn't make him jump through hoops. The father didn't give him advice or options. He simply gave his son the money that belonged to him.

The son spent it all on wild living, ended up in a pigpen, and came back to himself. I think about how the father released and blessed him, even though he knew it wasn't the right decision. He empowered the young son to find out for himself that everything that he needed was in his father's house. When the leaders in my life released me in the same way, and I went for a couple of weeks, I just began to see things that confirmed what they said.

I'm an Enneagram one, so reality is very important to me. My hypocrisy meter was on. Not that I was overly critical, but I was just paying attention to things. I felt an uneasiness, and the plans changed. We were going out to lunch—I had all my stuff in a U-Haul already. I was already packed up. They blessed me, had a party, and gave me a cake; "He's leaving, woo!" Students were crying because I'd just become the youth pastor which is what I'd wanted the whole time. It wasn't a paid position, but I was just so excited to be able to do that. It's what I had been praying for.

But then this opportunity came, and so I was ready to go. I'd made my decision—I had to stick with it, even if I was still uncertain at this point. I was stepping by faith. What I learned is that sometimes it takes faith to step out, but it also takes faith to stay put.

There was a prophet who had just been at the church—born in Singapore, very prophetic—and asked one of my fellow pastors and me to come meet him at the airport for a meal. We didn't want to leave this gentleman, who was a friend of my fellow pastor's dad, at the airport. So we went out to eat with this guy. The first thing he said when he got in the car was, "Pastor Mike, this young man is going to really help you build the church really well."

Pastor Mike said, "Well, Mike's leaving. He's moving. Going to . . . " And he went silent. It was an awkward silence. I could hear the man's wheels spinning.

Later, at the lunch table, he told us about his journey and his desire to have a big ministry—to do miracles and crusades. He got to work hand in hand with his heroes. But he became very disappointed because the closer he got to some of them, the more he realized that they were impressive from far off but not up close. They treated their wives like dirt. They were cruel to their staffs. That just broke his heart. But eventually, he had a big ministry, and did some miracles and crusades. But he became more enamored with the miracles and the crowd and the ministry and the glory than he did with his walk with God and caring about people.

He came to a place in his life where he was broke, and he said, "I don't care whom I work with or where you have me, God. If you want me to clean toilets in Jamaica, I'll go." At this point in the conversation, Pastor Mike excused himself to the restroom. I was praying sincerely and deeply, "God, if you have a word for me, please tell me."

This prophet didn't know that I was going into huge ministry, but he looked at me and asked, "Did God give you a word to leave?" Because of my pride, I didn't say anything. I just looked at him. The man continued, "Here's why. Because if God didn't give you a word to go, and you go, you'll step up from under grace, you'll be living in sin, and you'll wander in the wilderness. And what would've taken you one year here, will take you ten years there, and you'll end up in the same place. So if you have a word from God, go, and if you don't have a word from God, stay put."

I knew immediately what to do. I thanked him for being so transparent and honest, and I really was grateful. Then I told Dr. Jones, " I will never leave this place again unless you bless me. I'm taking that weight off of my shoulders and trusting you with my next—if there is one." I thought it was on me to fulfill my destiny, to position myself, and to take the opportunities. I didn't realize that weight was supposed to be on my spiritual father. And when God speaks to him, he's going to speak to me. And if He speaks to me, I'm going to confirm it through him because I've come up under His authority.

I submitted myself to him. And, it was so freeing! I could just focus on God, loving people, and serving the house. I served that vision as if it were my own. And I was ready to serve it until Jesus came back. That's the lesson I learned, and here's why I'm so passionate about it: Thirty days later I met Charla on a blind date. Sixty days later, Dr. Jones decided to offer me a part-time job at the church. Ninety days later, I was the youth pastor again—the people who had taken the position realized they weren't anointed for it. They said, "Hey, we feel like you're still the youth pastor. Would you please be the youth pastor; it's what the kids need." And I was also ordained.

Because of my submission and my willingness to die to self, a favor came upon my life and accelerated the vision in my life.

What happened in one year would've taken ten years out there. Because of my submission and my willingness to die to self, a favor came upon my life and accelerated the vision in my life. You don't have to be a rebel to make things happen in God's kingdom. You're going produce an Ishmael if you do it with a rebellious spirit. Wait for Isaac. God doesn't need your help to get you to your destiny; you simply need to surrender.

I do believe that God plants people out, of course. I believe God moves people from one local church to another, but there is a proper way and an order to that process, as well. How we leave one place is how we enter the next, so it's essential for every child of God to grasp this truth so that we can be honorable and flourish in the house of God. I believe in the power of agreement and alignment and assignments with God and with His people for His purpose.

We all have a belief system that contains a set of expectations—spoken and unspoken. If we're going to flourish in the house we have to deal with our BS (our belief system, of course—what did you think I was referring to?). What we believe matters, and it's a direct result of how we think. That's why God wants us to renew our minds according to His Word.

No matter if I believe that the law of gravity is real, it exists.

Beliefs are like the roots of a tree—you can't see them, but they're the most important part of a living thing. Your belief system isn't something people see, but what you believe is evidenced in your life. I want you to believe that you can be planted in the house of God and flourish in His courts like a palm tree and a cedar. What you believe about alignments is important to that.

Today, many people are so concerned about who they are over in the kingdom of God; however, it's more important who you're under than who you're over. Think about the story of Naomi and Ruth.

Naomi was married to a man named Elimelech. Elimelech left Bethlehem (which means "house of bread" or "house of God") to go to Moab (which represents the world). It's never good when you leave the house of God to do things your own way. Ten years went by, and both Elimelech and his two sons died. Naomi, Elimelech's wife, had two daughters-in-law: Orpah and Ruth. She told them, "You two go back to your families in Moab. I'm going back to Bethlehem: to the house of God." Let's take a look at what happens next in Ruth 1:14-17 (NLT):

> *And again they wept together, and Orpah kissed her*
> *mother-in-law good-bye. But Ruth clung tightly to Naomi.*
> *"Look," Naomi said to her, "your sister-in-law has gone back*
> *to her people and to her gods. You should do the same."*
> *But Ruth replied, "Don't ask me to leave you and turn back.*
> *Wherever you go, I will go; wherever you live, I will live. Your*

people will be my people, and your God will be my God. Wherever you die, I will die, and there I will be buried. May the LORD punish me severely if I allow anything but death to separate us!"

Ruth said, "I don't want to go back—I'm with you. I know I'm supposed to be in Bethlehem, too." She could have abandoned her mother-in-law as soon as the men in their family had passed on, but she understood the principle of inheriting honor. She made a decision to stay aligned with the right who because she knew that whom you're aligned with is even more important than what you're aligned with.

Maybe you're experiencing a down time in your life—maybe things are anything but good. I can totally relate to that.

When I was fourteen, I left the house of God to go into the world. I left the Father's house and headed straight for the pigpen like the prodigal son in Luke 15. I was far from God, and I was far from home. Even when I thought about going back to the house of God, the enemy had me believing that God was done with me. Just know that, no matter what your past, God still has great plans for you, and He loves you unconditionally. When you go back home, you will be met with His mercy and grace and healing love.

Ruth told Naomi that her God would be Ruth's God, too. Whom you align your life with is huge. "It's tremendous," Dr. Jones says, "You will be the same person in five years as you are today except for the people you meet and the books you read." I've always told my children, "If you show me your friends, I'll show you your future." Many of us have heard this

saying, too: "Birds of a feather flock together and they arrive together."
Whom you fly with determines how high you get. Aligning with the
right people is vital to setting yourself up for your next best thing.

When God wants to bless you, He brings a person into your life. The
enemy wants to harm you, and He also brings people into your life,
so whom we choose to do life with determines what's ahead for us—
blessing or harm. Choose wisely. Your next thing can be your best thing
when you are aligned with the right people—not perfect people, just
people who have a desire to dwell in the house of God.

Naomi and Ruth went back to Bethlehem during harvest time. Notice
that we never hear about Orpah again. Naomi gave Ruth instructions
to go into the fields of others and pick up the leftover harvest. Ruth
didn't push back on this. She listened and honored the authority in her
life—the godly authority that loved her. She could have said, "I'll go
pick up mine, but I'm not picking up yours too. You can get out there
too—you're not crippled!"

Naomi left Bethlehem on top, as a wealthy person. However, when
she returned to the house of God, they had nothing. They come back
because they realized everything they could ever need was in the house
of God. Ruth listened to Naomi, humbled herself, and responded to the
voice in her life with, "Yes. I will do that." Remember, humility precedes
honor, and it takes humility to honor the voices in our life even when
we don't agree with them.

While Ruth was there gathering, she caught the eye of the field owner, Boaz, who started to watch her. Because she was rightfully aligned, she was put in the sight of the right person. What a powerful kingdom principle to remember: there is always someone watching you who has the power to bless you.

Boaz was attracted to her, yes, but he was also impressed by the honor she showed to her mother-in-law. So, too, is God attracted to us when we honor those we are supposed to be in alignment with. I believe faithfulness matters—faithfulness to God, to the right people, to the right voice.

Boaz saw Ruth and told her to stay in his field. He blessed her, and she carried a plentiful harvest back to Naomi. Boaz is a symbol of God to us—even what we do "in secret," He sees, and He will reward us openly. Be faithful to what He has said, to align with whom He says, and do little things with excellence and a heart of honor.

Naomi echoed Boaz's instructions to Ruth not to go into another field. Both voices agreed, setting Ruth up for her next best thing! The right voice matters! God's delegated authority over us is never intended to hurt, abuse, or control us but rather to help us reach levels we can only reach by standing on their shoulders. When we are aligned with the right people and voices, it will take us far beyond our degrees and résumés ever could. If you will apply this principle faithfully, God will make sure your next thing is your best thing— better than your last thing.

> When we are aligned with the right people and voices, it will take us far beyond our degrees and résumés ever could.

Ruth found favor in faithfulness. So will you with your employer. Your boss is looking to promote and pay more to someone who can advance the company. It was the same with Boaz and it's the same with God who is watching how we honor and value those in our lives and how we are advancing the kingdom of God. This is a principle I teach men in our church. We need to align with the right men in friendship. Most men don't have a best friend. But the Bible, in Proverbs 27:17 (NLT), tells us that "iron sharpens iron." We need others who will sharpen us. Who's sharpening you?

The way Boaz felt about Ruth is the way God feels about us. Be faithful in your field—whether you're a student, employee, volunteer, financial giver, etc. You may not like it, but all things are working together. Ruth's faithfulness paid off big time, and so will yours.

Naomi's next instruction to her daughter-in-law was to go to Boaz. They end up getting married—another blessing of alignment and right voice. Now the field she'd once begged in would be hers! She had no idea when she first stepped foot into it. Likewise, I had no idea the church I was saved in, served in, and was on staff at would one day be the church I stewarded.

Boaz redeemed Ruth. It's the same with Jesus Christ. He sees and knows what you've been through. And when we honor and say yes to the right alignments that He leads us into, He will bless us and promote us. We will be fruitful, stable, durable, and useful for His kingdom purposes.

No matter what has happened in your past, believe that God still has a great **PLAN** for your future.

Believe that **WHOM** you align with **NOW** is more important than where you have been.

Believe that **FAITHFULNESS** matters.

Believe there is a **PURPOSE** in your now for your **NEXT BEST**.

There are alignments in assignments—in the right *whos*. I think about these dynamic duos:

> ⤳ Moses and Joshua
> ⤳ Elijah and Elisha—Elisha served Elijah and never left his side even when Elijah tested his heart to see if he would leave or stay with the prophets at school. Take a look at 2 Kings 2:2:

> *"The Lord has told me to go to Bethel."*
> *But Elisha replied, "As surely as the LORD lives and*
> *you yourself live, I will never leave you!"*
> *So they went down together to Bethel.*

You might be thinking, *That's all well and good when the leader over someone is healthy . . . but what about when a leader is* unhealthy?

Let's take a look at Saul and David. Saul was emotionally and spiritually unhealthy, abusing and threatening David on multiple occasions. David fled but still honored his king. We don't need to stay under unhealthy, insecure, abusive leadership, but we do need to honor them with our words and attitudes. We do need to humbly appeal, as David did, to the Lord and pray for our leaders. When we do, God will ensure that we get to our next best thing—even if our last thing was our worst thing.

And if that is your praying on behalf of leadership in the house of God, I want to say I'm sorry. These can be some of the most painful experiences we have in our relationships, but just know that what the devil meant for evil God can use for good. Even when things are good, God is still in your story. It's not over yet. Stay in honor, stay prayerful, and watch what God can do. Don't give up on God, don't give up on the house of God, and don't give up on being a part of a local church and leadership. There are great leaders and pastors that God is raising up who are not perfect but who are absolute gifts in the body of Christ and in our lives.

CHAPTER 7

SPARKS WILL FLY

As iron sharpens iron, so one person sharpens another.

—Proverbs 27:17 (NIV)

I remember the first time I was using jumper cables on my car as a sixteen-year-old. Don't laugh—but I was not prepared for what happened. I knew there was a black handle and a red handle—and that's about all I knew. I didn't realize the power of a positive and a negative charge coming together. So as I figured out how to connect the red handle to the red knob on my friend's car battery and the black handle to the black knob, I didn't realize that no longer could the other red and black handle touch. Boy, was I shocked when I accidentally put them in one hand to walk to my car! Sparks flew. I screamed and fell to the ground. I figured out really quickly what can happen when a positive and a negative come into contact with each other.

It's the same way in relationships. Challenges and conflicts are inevitable, whether they be in marriage, family, friendships, businesses, or churches. Many times, we avoid conflict. While it's never fun, it is necessary for us to grow. It's kind of like when a person goes to work out at the gym; it doesn't make sense in the natural to pick up weights that are heavy and lift them. However, what happens when a person picks up a dumbbell? They embrace the tension. They begin to do curls, and they force blood into their muscle on purpose. The muscles break down, and there's pain involved, but there's a saying you may have heard before in the gym: "No pain, no gain." After the muscle is broken down, it is repaired by the body and built up again stronger and bigger.

This is a beautiful picture of us as the body of Christ embracing tension, facing conflict, forcing conversation, and focusing on our issues. We've got to break it down so that we can bring healing and repair, be stronger, be more mature, and grow up in Christ. When it comes to a positive and a negative, here's what I believe: when we bring positivity to a negative situation, we can see true power and change. That's why being positive is so important as a child of God—because nothing positive can happen when I get negative. Even when there's negative conflict, if I approach it in humility and faith with positivity, sparks may fly, but power will be released so that we can move forward into God's best purpose for our lives, our families, and our churches.

Remember . . .

> - The *Great Calling* is to be fruitful and multiply.
> - The *Great Commandment* is to love God and love people.
> - The *Great Commission* is to reach people and help them become fully devoted followers of Jesus Christ.

As noted in previous chapters, all of these involve God and people. God brings people into our lives that irritate us—much like when a piece of sand gets inside of an oyster and begins to irritate it, friction eventually produces a pearl. We need people in our lives who may irritate us for our good so that we can produce pearls: things of great value. God says that, when believers come together, good things can happen. As we connect in community and in discipleship, things can get heated and sparks will fly. But think about this concept: one person sharpens another. In order to get sharper, we first have to come together. We have to connect—and there's going to be friction there. It's going to get heated. But if we stay connected even in the heat, we will be better.

Have you ever heard of the phrase "rubbed the wrong way"? If we are going to become the best version of ourselves, we will need to embrace the idea of being rubbed the wrong way. Many times, our way of thinking is, *I don't want anybody to rub me the wrong way.*

Don't misunderstand what I'm saying—I don't *want* to be rubbed the wrong way, but there are seasons in my life in which I *need* to be rubbed the wrong way so that God can smooth out the rough edges in my life and in my character.

Recently, when hearing about someone's experience at our church for the first time as a volunteer, I heard this statement: "I had an unpleasant experience. This person rubbed me the wrong way." I overheard this in another conversation regarding the experience, and it dawned on me. Often, we come into a place like a local church with unrealistic expectations—we assume that we're dealing with a highly trained, fully functional organization when, in reality, it is a group of diverse people with diverse backgrounds and experiences that are in different places in their spiritual journey and are at different levels of maturity and people skills. We expect that there should never be any errors or mistakes. Wouldn't you agree that this is an unfair and unrealistic expectation? It's amazing how we can walk into a local church and desire to be overwhelmed with undeserved grace and mercy but then struggle to actually extend the same to others.

That's why it's so important for us to embrace humility, lean into Jesus, and be filled with His love, grace, and mercy—not only for ourselves, but to extend to others as they will often need it. Could it be that this is why Jesus, in the Lord's Prayer in Matthew 6:12, said, "Father, forgive us of our [transgressions] as we forgive those who [transgress] against us"—because not only do we need it but so do others? If and when unrealistic expectations are not met, people will leave the house of God—the very place where their lives can be forever changed, where they can flourish. My prayer is that we will learn to mature to new levels of intimacy with God and with each other.

CONFLICT RESOLUTION

If we are going to flourish in the house of God and in relationships, it's important that we learn and understand and put into practice biblical principles of conflict resolution. As one of my mentors has taught me, conflict has a last name: resolution.

> If we are going to flourish in the house of God and in relationships, it's so important that we learn and understand and put into practice biblical principles of conflict resolution.

Many friendships, families, marriages, businesses, and churches have never learned how to live out conflict resolution skills by faith. But we are getting better, and I believe that's where we need to rest our hope and faith when it comes to the local church. Jesus is building His church and coming back for a bride who has made herself ready. And she will make herself ready as we embrace humility, deny ourselves, become filled with God's Holy Spirit, and mature into the stature of Christ.

Again, this goes back to unrealistic expectations. If we are in relationship, there will be conflict—it's unrealistic to believe that there won't be. I think God made it to be that way so that we could learn patience, forgiveness, mercy, longsuffering, and courage. Conflict is hard. And people who want it concern me a little. But most of us avoid it, and when we don't address it, that space always fills up with negativity, and the enemy begins to create a narrative that can bring division and skew our perspective, causing us to believe half-truths.

Jesus wants us to address conflict immediately—so that we don't give the enemy any room to create a wrong narrative. The enemy wants us to keep it in secrecy and darkness because that's how evil thrives, but Jesus wants us to bring into the light so that it can be identified, confessed, repented of, and reconciliation can happen—which is the goal of conflict resolution. What we may not realize about conflict resolution is that it is a doorway to deeper intimacy. Whether your fights growing up were with your best friend, a brother, or a sister, after the conflict there was forgiveness, confession, and repentance that led you to go deeper in your relationship.

This is true when it comes to marriage. I did not have great conflict resolution skills growing up because it wasn't modeled for me— nor was it model for my parents. I wanted to become better—to learn from my history so that I would not repeat it. I committed to becoming a learner of great marriages, observing them from afar and even getting up close to learn firsthand how to have successful family relationships. When Charla and I began, in our early years, I didn't realize there would be any conflict because we loved each other so much . . . boy, was I wrong.

When I was growing up, the way conflict resolution was modeled was loud yelling and shouting: if it got really escalated, stuff would break. I remember my first Christmas with my new bride—she had an expectation that I was going to drop everything on my day off and do all of the Christmas decorations in one afternoon. This was not my expectation—and yes, I thought it was unrealistic. It caused tension and, as a young twenty-eight-year-old still growing in my maturity, I remember not addressing the conflict. Finally, it built up to the point that I exploded and threw our Christmas tree across the room, breaking Charla's porcelain manger scene. Can I tell you how bad I felt? Not only did I allow anger and my lack of communication ability to result in a demonstration that did not glorify God or honor my wife—but I broke baby Jesus! I knew then I had room for growth—as I do today. I'm still committed to the growth process.

Lack of conflict resolution skills doesn't just exist in marriages—there's also a deficit of these skills in businesses which translates to an annual loss of $359 billion.[5] So, if we can learn and grow in biblical conflict resolution skills, not only will it improve our marriages—it'll improve our businesses and our churches, which will spill out into the world.

John 17 was Jesus' prayer: that we would be one so that the world would know that the Father sent Him. When we learn to come together in

---

5 "8 Ways to Resolve Employee Conflict at Work," *Western Governors University*, 3 Aug. 2021, https://www.wgu.edu/blog/8-ways-resolve-employee-conflict2108.html#close.

agreement and alignment, the anointing flows for our assignment, and the world sees that Jesus is the Messiah. Jesus also said that the world would know we are His by our love for one another, which means not only do we need conflict resolution—we need *conflict reconciliation*. Sometimes, resolution focuses on the problem, while reconciliation focuses on the relationship.

Most of the time, conflict in relationships is a doorway to deeper intimacy—yet many of us don't walk through that door to enjoy deep, committed relationships. It is my observation that this area is largely overlooked in our discipleship programs within churches. It may not even seem spiritual but this is a game-changer. So I may have piqued your interest about some good conflict resolution skills. I'm a practical guy, and I like solutions: don't just tell me what I need to know, show me how to work it and use it. That being said, let me share a few practical principles I believe can help you improve your conflict reconciliation skills.

All conflict stems from one attitude.

James 4:1 (NCV) says, "Do you know where your fights and arguments come from? They come from the selfish desires that war within you."

There are two incorrect ways to deal with conflict resolution. The first is *blow up, and don't show up.* You want to resolve it as soon as possible. Guard against isolation in conflict. It's okay to allow for some space, but for a designated time, and never overnight. Men, let's take the lead here! Ephesians 4:26 (NLT) says, "Do not let the sun go down while you are still angry." The key is to *show up, but don't blow up*. Don't stuff it all down—one day, you'll explode and say, "It's over!" That's not reconciliation. Reconciliation says, "We would rather be tight than right." The truth is that conflict does not resolve itself. Time does not heal. Our hearts get harder, and our positions get more solidified.

When we avoid difficult conversations, we trade short-term discomfort for long-term dysfunction.

Few people resolve every issue. You're not going to agree on everything, but the relationship is more important to me than the issue. James 3:17 (TLB) says, "Wisdom . . . is peace-loving and courteous. It allows discussion and is willing to yield to others." It's wise to compromise. You can have unity without uniformity. We can walk hand in hand without seeing eye to eye. It simply takes effort—understanding others is not natural. But Philippians 2:4 instructs us to care about others as much as we care about ourselves.

One of the most powerful peace-making statements you can say is, "I'm sorry. I was wrong. Will you forgive me?" One verbal missile can tear apart and take away twenty acts of kindness. It is a 1 to 20 ratio—and women can remember forever! The tongue is so small yet so powerful. It's a two-ounce slab of mucous membrane that can maim, injure, and destroy. Think about toothpaste: once you squeeze the tube, you can't get it back in. Words are the same. This is why we must be sure that we're speaking to address the problem instead of attacking a person. We're all on the same team. We should use the right wording, saying things like, "When you do that, it makes me feel . . . " instead of, "You *always* do this and you *never* . . . !"

Once, Charla and I got into a heated disagreement, and I didn't confront the tension. I needed to be somewhere. We were arguing, and I left. I was in my car, venting to God, when He reminded me that it was the enemy—it was spiritual warfare. I called Charla and reminded her of the devil's role in our conflict. We repented, prayed, and it was totally resolved. We have the authority as believers to recognize the enemy's schemes by humbling ourselves, repenting, and saying, "I'm sorry." If we are going to have great relationships, we will have to be great apologizers and great forgivers.

You need to fight the devil, not people. Learn how to engage in spiritual warfare! I've already said this, but the enemy is a liar: he will plant lies into your head, so don't give him room! Know that he is working hard to destroy relationships, families, and churches. He doesn't want us to be fruitful and multiply. He doesn't want us growing, loving God and people—or reaching and discipling people.

Remember: there is *only one enemy*!

Ephesians 6:12 tell us that our fight is not against flesh and blood. Conflict will be messy and heated, but you can work it out and go to new level of intimacy in your relationship. Maybe today, in the middle of the conflict, ask yourself, *What do I do when it seems hopeless?* Before you go to your spouse or any other person, before you make that post or leave that church, talk to God about it. Vent vertically, not horizontally. Go to the *throne* before you go to the *phone*.

David modeled this for us in the Psalms: he gave his complaints to God first. In the New Testament, the apostle James wrote that "you have not because you ask not" (James 4:2, author paraphrase). We're going about conflict all wrong! How can we concentrate on reconciliation? By seeking to understand before seeking to be understood. One of the greatest conflict resolution tools ever is stating *their* side of the story to their satisfaction (Proverbs 18:13). Consider their perspective! And guard your tongue.

1 Peter 3:8-9 (NIV) says:

> *Finally, all of you, be like-minded, be sympathetic, love one another, be compassionate and humble. Do not repay evil with evil or insult with insult. On the contrary, repay evil with blessing because to this you were called so that you may inherit a blessing.*

Fight the real enemy, and call on God for help! God wants us to be healed, to feel free, and to share all that we are facing. Confess your sins to God and ask Him for forgiveness! Go to one another for healing. You can be totally loved by God and then give that love to each other; only God can be the source of this love!

If we are going to flourish in the house of God, we should invoke the help of the Holy Spirit and apply God's Word by faith to bring resolution to conflict. When we do, we will be sharper and better. I believe we will grow in so many ways and bring forth mature fruit that emulates the fragrance of Christ.

Unity is where God commands the blessing according to Psalm 133. When we are unified, it is beautiful to God, and it's where the anointing flows to the whole body of Christ. May we choose the way to unity and see the power of God flowing in us and through us in our families, relationships, and churches, shining with the Glory of God that testifies to the world that Jesus is the Christ!

> **When we are unified, it is beautiful to God, and it's where the anointing flows to the whole body of Christ.**

CHAPTER 8

THE REAL "F" WORD

When people think about the state of our world today, they want to know, "Pastor, is this the end? I mean, are we in the end-times? Is Jesus coming back?"

I believe that we're in what Jesus called the *beginning* of the end—the beginning of birth pains. There have been a lot of birth pains this year in our nation. There'd be some intensity, some swelling, and then it would fall back. But Jesus' own disciples asked Him the same thing two thousand years ago: "Jesus, you talk about coming back—when are you coming back?" And so He began to walk through this exhaustive list of some things to look for before He returns. I want to point to this passage, found in Matthew 24:10-12 (NLT) because what He says is stunning: "And many will turn away from me and betray and hate each other. . . . Sin will be rampant everywhere. And the love of many will grow cold."

Now, when we look around, I think we can agree that sin is running wild. I mean, it's off the chain. As believers, we should not be shocked by that—it's the world system. We know that those who don't follow Christ live that way. But in this passage, Jesus is not talking about unbelievers. He's talking about those who have turned to Him. See, you can't turn away from Him unless you've turned to Him.

Jesus also said that the love of many will grow cold—he's talking about the *agape*, the God kind of love, that you can't receive unless you've turned to Jesus and believed on Him. This is referring to the church. Jesus said that many will turn away from Him. Therefore, it's possible for those of us who have trusted Christ, who've believed on Him, who have the power and the work of the Holy Spirit in our lives, to have love that grows cold. That should be kind of a warning! This should be a checkup. As one of my pastors used to say, "a checkup from the neck up."

Maybe you're sitting there thinking, *How can my love grow cold?* One of the major ways is getting offended. We live in what's called a cancel culture. People are getting more offended more rapidly than ever. It means, "I'm cutting you off if you don't agree with me, if you do something I don't like." Some people become so offended that they go from 0 to 100 in rage. Look at what Jesus said in Luke 17:1 (author paraphrase): "It is impossible for offenses not to come." He's saying, "Listen. You're whacked if you do; you're whacked if you don't." Offenses are going to come your way. They have come, they are here, and they will come again, o the question isn't whether the offense is going to come. The question is how will we respond? Jesus wants us to learn this truth from kingdom culture today.

I want to give us a biblical response to offense. In the last couple of years, if you haven't been offended, you haven't been breathing because offenses have come from everywhere. You can say one thing that sets somebody off. I'm not fearful of that. I think it's just a great opportunity for us as believers to know this. It's important that I understand how to be intentional about dealing with offense, so the love of God can flow through me in forgiveness—because the world needs the *agape* of God. And if I'm holding on to offense, then it becomes a hindrance to the love of God flowing through me to a world that so desperately needs it.

So what is an offense? Let's think about this. It's the Greek word *skandalon*. What is that? Maybe you grew up watching *Bugs Bunny*. If you remember Elmer Fudd, he was always trying to get that wascally wabbit, right? Have you seen the episode where he puts a box with a little stick and a string? He gets behind a tree and puts some carrots in there. Well, that's actually an ancient hunting technique called a *skandalon* where the hunter puts bait under a trap and then discreetly goes off to the side and hopes that an animal comes up, takes the bait, and gets trapped. It's the same word we see here.

Jesus said that an offense can be a trap for believers. John Bevere wrote a great book called *The Bait of Satan*. I highly recommend it. We have to be intentional about dealing with offense. And here's the thing about offense: we're most prone to offense by the people closest to us. Because, again, there's this thing called expectation.

Let me give you the two sides of expectation. When you're in relationship with someone, you have expectations of what they should do and shouldn't do. When they do what you expect them to do, you can be tempted to become ungrateful. That's why we can take people for granted, even when they're meeting our expectations. Here's the other side of expectation: you don't do what I expected, and I become disappointed and offended. So offense is a trap that the enemy uses to keep the love of God from flowing to us and, ultimately, through us. Proverbs 18:19 (NLT) says, "An offended friend is harder to win back than a fortified city. Arguments separate friends, like a gate locked with bars."

I don't control what happens to me, but I do control what happens inside of me. An offense, the Bible says, is like a gate. Or think about it this way: "Offense equals a fence." When I become offended, if I don't properly deal with it, I can figuratively begin to build a fence around my heart and my life as self-preservation. But what I don't understand in doing so is that not only am I keeping you out—I'm keeping God out. And it's behind the bars of offense that my love begins to grow cold. I have the control and the power to recognize it and not let it happen. But typically, in our pain and our hurt, we begin to build the fence, and we act like it doesn't bother us. Our heart becomes hardened. And then we find ourselves not trusting people, withholding our love, etc. What we're doing is hardening our heart. And the *agape* love of God begins to grow cold. Jesus said that it's impossible that offenses wouldn't come. It's going to happen. So what are you going to do when they come?

Maybe you've been offended. Maybe you've been canceled. I know what that's like. There are people who have left our church after 10 or 15 years of life change over one issue—my heart goes out to that. That's not something that I like, but it's wrong of me to be offended by that and act as if it doesn't hurt me. Because there's a part of me, having been left and abandoned as a young man, as a young boy, and a child, that is tempted to harden my heart and say, "Go ahead, leave. You wanna walk out? Other people have walked out. Go ahead!" However, now I'm building offense, and the love of God will grow cold in me. So I cannot allow that to take root in my heart.

Maybe there's been an offense in your life. Maybe somebody walked out on you, betrayed you, said they loved you and got close to you, found out that you weren't perfect, and then abandoned you. Maybe it was a spouse who cheated on you. Maybe they've gone on and started another life—maybe another family. And you find yourself offended. Canceled. Or maybe a boss didn't recognize your potential—and not only did he not give you a promotion, but he cut you this year. It was a very difficult decision, you are offended by that person, and you're holding on to what they did to you or what they didn't do for you.

Maybe somebody you're in a relationship with made this statement: "Black lives matter." Maybe you said, "All lives matter," and you took a stance, offended. Maybe the issue was, "Should we shut the church down or keep the church open?" You say, "Well, I think we ought to open it up. If we had faith, we'd open the church." Others say, "Well, if we cared about people, we'd close it down." What are we going do? We make a decision, but yet you find yourself offended in the very place God changed your life. Maybe it's something like, "Should I wear a mask or no mask?" "Well," some say, "if you had faith, you wouldn't have to wear a mask."

Maybe it was an issue like these that set you off, and now you've canceled a friend—or maybe even somebody in your family. Maybe it was an issue over voting: Biden or Trump? We want to know because we think, *I can't even do kingdom culture with you if you're not lining up with everything I believe.* God's trying to bring us to a place of maturity where we're not so taken by what's happening in our world and our culture, where we're saying, "Hey, you have the right to do that. I'm going to love you anyway, and I'm going to do kingdom with you. I'm not going to allow the *agape* love in my life to grow cold over an earthly issue. I'm not going to do it."

I'm not going to allow the **agape** love in my
life to grow cold over an earthly issue.

This is what we look like to God: We're trying to worship God, and there is a fence. We're trying to get closer to God, but we can't. We're trying to love people, but we find ourselves captured behind a wall of apathy and hardened hearts. When we are offended, that spirit will actually attract facts to back up a narrative that causes us to believe that we're still right. And here's the thing we need to be humble enough about: each and every one of us can be wrong and still *think* we're right.

That's why the Bible calls it deception. This enemy of ours is a master deceiver. He will come to us and try to get us to believe a certain way, and we will build a stronghold of how we think about this one thing. The demonic hides out in that stronghold, and we cannot even recognize that our thinking isn't lining up with the Word of God. This is how our love grows cold. So, we've got to ask ourselves, *Am I offended? Has my love grown cold?*

I want to offer you three steps for cancel offenses. Love cancels offenses.

In Matthew 6:41-12 (author paraphrase), Jesus said, "Why do you look at the speck in your brother's eye, but do not consider the plank in your own eye? Or how can you say to your brother, let me remove that speck from your eye, and look, a plank is in your own eye. You hypocrite. First, remove the plank from your own eye, and then you will see clearly to remove the speck from your brother's eye."

In order for me to step away from being offended, for me to be free, *I've got to pull the plank from my own eye*. I'm walking around, and I don't even realize that it's there. I'm so focused on the speck in your eye, but God says I have to deal with the plank in my own eye first. Here's what happens when I pull it out: I gain perspective. As a young twenty-something, I looked at the condition of my life and blamed it all on my dad. But when I came to Christ, I realized I had a plank in my own eye. The Holy Spirit said, *Michael, you made the choices you made, with or without your dad.* Only after I pulled out the plank was I able to properly see my dad as God did.

Here's the second thing. *I've got to pull down the stronghold of a fence in my life.* I've got to pull down the way I think about that situation or that person. I'm going to deconstruct because I've just decided that that issue isn't worth my freedom. And when it comes to eternal matters, just ask yourself this: the thing you're offended about, in eternity, does it even really matter? And if it doesn't, let it go. We're going to pick up our cross. It's here that I remembered it was my offenses that put Jesus on the cross. And it's here that I bring those offenses to the foot of the cross where I first felt His love and found His grace and mercy. I had offended God, yet God forgave me. And it's at the bloodstained cross of Christ that I now must pick up my cross and follow Jesus. He said, "If you lay down your life and pick up your cross and follow me, you're going to discover true life." So put down the fence. Pick up your cross.

Here's the third one: *Pray for your offender. How can I do that?* you may wonder. I realized, after a little while following Jesus, that pain shaped me into the person I am today. In Genesis 50, Joseph's brother's discover that the ruler in front of them is the brother they'd tried to kill and sold into slavery. Look at what Joseph said: "Don't be afraid. Am I in the place of God? Am I God that I can punish you? What you meant for evil, God turned it into my good. And now I've helped save the lives of many people" (vv. 19-20, author paraphrase).

Through the misery you have felt, God can bring forth great ministry. God will take that pain and turn it into a platform. That's why you can offer forgiveness and pray for those who have hurt you and wounded you—because the enemy meant it for evil to defeat you, but God is going to turn it around to develop you into a man or woman of faith who has this compassion and love.

We see Jesus living this out: Luke 6:28 (NLT) says, "Bless those who curse you. Pray for those who hurt you." And then we see Jesus on the cross exemplify this very teaching. The God who created the earth and the people in it was crucified by the very people He came to save. Jesus' last temptation was to be offended. He was hanging there, and they began to mock Him. This was the enemy's last attempt to get Jesus to hold on to the bitterness and offense. But Jesus said in Luke 23:34 (author paraphrase), "Father, forgive them because they don't even know what they're doing."

Maybe today, you just need to come into agreement with the cross. The pain is real. But God is going to turn that thing into good. God is going to bring purpose out of your pain. Forgiveness isn't saying that what they did was okay. It's saying that we're not going to punish them for it. That's why Joseph said, "Am I God? Can I punish you? No I can't. God is the judge. Vengeance belongs to God." If I stay in love and offer forgiveness, I create space for God to do what only God can do.

Are you offended today? Maybe the love of God has grown cold in your life. Maybe you need to come back to the cross and let the love of God stir your heart. Maybe today you need to forgive somebody—because that's what Jesus says to you when you look to Him: "I forgive you." Don't turn away from the Holy Spirit. Turn to Him! Let this be a turning point for you today. Come out of that offense and the trap that the enemy set for you. And as you look to Jesus today, listen: He's never going to reject you. You will always find mercy when you come humbly to Him.

If we don't allow God to transform our pain, we will transmit it. People can hurt us, but God can also heal us through people. Healed people heal people. Hurt people hurt people. You don't have to hurt anymore. You can be healed and allow God to transmit healing through your life to all who are around you. This is what the Healer wants to do—in your heart and life, family, marriage, children, business, school, community, and the world!

You are forgiven, so be free, and extend that same forgiveness to your offender. God wants you to be healed, so you can be a vessel of healing to others.

SECTION THREE

THE PURPOSE OF GOD

CHAPTER 9
SHIFT HAPPENS

In the beginning, God created man in His own image in a garden. Do you remember what He created Adam from? The soil—the dirt. He made man in His own image and put him in a garden with the instruction to be fruitful and multiply.

God is constantly talking about this idea of being fruitful and multiplying. He has designed you to flourish. He *wants* you to flourish. There are a lot of people who get critical because they struggle with that—as if you should be suffering, sick, angry, discouraged, and defeated, or else you're not really holy. But that wasn't Jesus! If Jesus had been like that, kids wouldn't have run up to him. Think about it: kids don't run up to people who aren't friendly or welcoming or warm.

Here's the definition of flourish again according to *Merriam-Webster*: "to grow luxuriantly, to thrive, to achieve success, to prosper, to be in a state of activity or production, to reach a height of development." God wants His church, His kingdom, and His family to flourish because it's a demonstration to the world of who He is. He wants to show the heavenly realms the wisdom of God through the church.

> God wants His church, His kingdom,
> and His family to flourish because it's a
> demonstration to the world of who He is.

So how do we do this according to His will, His plan, and His purpose? God placed a seed of greatness on the inside of you from the time that you were born. But how do we see it manifest in our lives? Is it possible to be a believer and a follower of Christ but never really flourish? I think it is. There is a process, a plan, an order to the way we see this manifest in our lives.

Psalm 92:12-14 (AMP) says:

> *The righteous will flourish like the date palm [long-lived,*
> *upright and useful]. They will grow like a cedar in Lebanon*
> *[majestic and stable]. Planted in the house of the LORD,*
> *They will flourish in the courts of our God. [Growing in grace] they*
> *will still thrive and bear fruit and prosper in old age; They will flourish*
> *and be vital and fresh [rich in trust and love and contentment].*

Does that sound good to you? However, I can't flourish and be fruitful until I'm planted. That's why the enemy works so hard to get believers disconnected from a local church. In order to get planted, I may have to give a shift. Because shift happens. What do I have to shift? I have to shift how I think. I have to shift how I live. I have to shift what I value—anything that I have is in direct correlation to what I think and what I do.

Think about Psalm 23 (AMP). We usually hear it at funeral services and gravesides, right? It always has this "death" feel to it for me: "Though I walk through the valley of the shadow of death, I will fear no evil. . . ." But I want to look at it from a different perspective: you're alive here on the earth. Let's read it.

> *The LORD is my Shepherd [to feed, to guide and to shield me],*
> *I shall not want.*
> *He lets me lie down in green pastures;*

This speaks of *shalom*—peace!

He leads me beside the still and quiet waters.
He refreshes and restores my soul (life);
He leads me in the paths of righteousness
for His name's sake.

In other words, He's teaching me the right way of living—the God-first life.

Even though I walk through the [sunless] valley of the shadow of death,

Death is in the future—it will happen.

I fear no evil, for You are with me;
Your rod [to protect] and Your staff [to guide],
they comfort and console me.
You prepare a table before me in the presence of my enemies.
You have anointed and refreshed my head with oil;
My cup overflows.

If I can add to the Amplified Version, I'd put "flourishing" in parentheses here. I don't want to tap into the reserves; I want to tap into the overflow!

Surely goodness and mercy and unfailing love
shall follow me all the days of my life,
And I shall dwell forever [throughout all my days] in
the house and in the presence of the LORD.

Notice the note there that says, "Throughout all my days"? In other words, you're not going to have all these benefits in heaven. I want dwell in the house of the Lord *all the days of my life*. So many people have limited the house of God to a steeple—a brick building—the little Christmas globe with snow that plays music and has ice skaters out on the little frozen little mirror in front of the steeple. But we know that the house of God is the presence of God with the people of God living in the purpose of God.

It's always been the presence, the people, and the purpose. It started as Adam and Eve, the people, in the presence of God and the purpose of God. What was the purpose? To be fruitful and multiply. Then it was Noah and his family, people of God, with the presence of God, fulfilling the purpose of God: build the ark, go through the storm, be fruitful and multiply. Then it was Moses and Israel, the people of God, with the presence of God, fulfilling the purpose of God: get from the land of not enough to the land of more than enough. Then it was David and his family, the people of God, in the presence of God, fulfilling the purpose of God: David's lineage created a pipeline for the Messiah.

Then we see Jesus hit the scene; for 400 years, there had been silence, but Jesus cleared the temple. Passion for God's house consumed Him! He was restoring what was lost, the presence of God had arrived. We see Jesus with disciples, the people of God, fulfilling the purpose of God. In Acts 2, Jesus is in heaven, but now the Holy Spirit comes, the presence of God, with 120 people of God. Peter preaches, three thousand get saved, and the church is birthed—the purpose of God.

You can't just have one of the three elements. Some people are trying to have only the presence of God. "It's just me and Jesus." I'm not a big fan of church on demand. Why? Because it's church at your convenience. I'm just not sure you can really serve God's purpose in your life *conveniently*. Remember, worship is a sacrifice. You can't flourish in life without the presence of God, the people of God, and the purpose of God.

One benefit of being planted in the house is that God's favor and mercy follow you all the days of your life. His goodness and His mercy flow from His favor. And when I shift into position, I get planted to flourish with favor. Here's the definition of favor: a position. It's a position from which kindly acts proceed to provide you with special advantages: preferential treatment. Favor is awesome. Favor is your having an access to a room you've never been in before and a pastor comes up and says, "Hey, Michael, how you doing, man? I'm flying to Atlanta on Friday. You should stay an extra day and fly with me on my private jet." We never know when the favor's coming. That's why we got to stay in position.

That's why the enemy tries to get people out of position because position is a divine advantage for success. Favor can cause acceleration. Favor can change everything in twenty-four hours. And when I'm planted, I will flourish with favor. Even though my enemies come at me, He's going to guide me, protect me, and prepare a table in the midst of my enemies to watch the goodness of God play out in my life and in my favor—they will see shift happen.

December is an axis month. In December, the earth is the farthest away from the sun. It holds the darkest day of the year. But then, in June, there's another axis month: another shift. The earth goes around the sun, and there's a heat shift. The earth leans toward the sun. That's why we get better tans and it gets hotter. The downside is that it gets humid, and those pesky little mosquitoes come out. But the bottom line is that the earth turns a corner.

If God wants us to be fruitful and multiply, He wants to bless us. He wants us to expand His name and His family in the earth. John 10:10 (author paraphrase) says, "The thief comes to steal, kill, and destroy." Jesus said, "I have come that they may have life and have it in abundance to the full 'til it overflows." But again, many people are not experiencing this piece of God's purpose for their lives. Could it be that it's because they're not in position? You're closer to a shift than you know, but sometimes, you quit and get out of position when favor is just around the corner.

Here's what shift means: "to transfer, move position, or reposition." Maybe you need a shift in your health, career, purpose, marriage, kids, or finances. Maybe you feel stuck. But I believe, as we get positioned, there's a shift that's going to take place.

Once, my daughter Madelyn and I were getting ice cream—she was probably about eight years old. Bruster's used to make this flavor called white chocolate raspberry truffle—vanilla with raspberry swirl and these dark chocolate chunks in it. Man, it was awesome in a waffle cone. The night we were in line was a hot August evening. Madelyn and I were up next when this car pulled into a handicap spot and a large, older gentleman got out without acknowledging anybody. He walked right up to the empty window, leaned in and started giving his order. Little Madelyn looked up at me to see how her dad was going to respond to this. I saw that one of his legs was abnormally large. I turned to Madelyn and said, "It's okay. Let's just let him go."

Sure, I was frustrated, but I tried to position myself, have a good witness for my daughter. This lady beside me tapped me on the arm and said, "Listen: why don't you go before me?" It was that simple. You can be in position, and somebody else can cut in front of you. It's easy to get discouraged, negative, or bitter. But never forget that there's always somebody watching you who has the power to bless you.

A shift in God's favor can happen. But if we get negative, we get out of position.

A shift in God's favor can happen. But if we get negative, we get out of position. So stay in faith, knowing God is going to shift your situation. One touch of His favor can shift everything. You don't need everybody to like you; you just need the right person to like you. You might be at a lower position at work, but then a shift happens. One break, one idea, one person, and God can shift favor into your life. I love what pastor Phil Munsey taught me: "That's why you need to treat every person like they're the gatekeeper to your destiny—because one day, you'll be right."

The people of God had been enslaved for four hundred years. They'd been mistreated, worked long hours, given no rest, and provided no food. But in one day, God brought them out with the wealth of Egypt. Exodus 3:22 (author paraphrase), says, "God said, 'Ask your neighbors for their gold and for their jewelry.'" God gave them favor with the Egyptians so that they walked out of Egypt with the wealth of Egypt. They plundered the nation in one day of God's favor.

Joseph was in a prison cell one moment in prison clothes. Twenty-four hours later, after he interpreted Pharaoh's dream, he was in the palace in palace clothes, second-in-command. No one can stop what God wants to bring into your life. That's why we've got to stay planted in His presence, with His people and His purpose. Stop worrying about haters who are trying to hold you back. In fact, sometimes, when people leave your life, it's proof that they're not called to the next level of your life. So don't get so upset. Stay in faith. Expect a shift to happen, and know that it's going to work out in your favor.

Isaiah 61:2 (NLT) says, "He sent me to tell those who mourn that the time of the LORD' s favor has come." David said God's favor is for a lifetime. Jesus announced in Luke 4:18-19 (NLT), quoting Isaiah, "The spirit of the LORD is upon me . . . and the time of the LORD's favor has come." So Jesus proclaimed that favor is here right now. I've just got to get positioned, to get into the flow of favor. I've got to believe it. I've got to declare it. I've got to expect it.

When God's favor happens, it's going to be big, and it's happening more quickly than you ever dreamed. It's going to be more rewarding than you expected. Position is everything. I used to coach my kids when they were younger, and even when they went into middle school and high school ball. When someone is shooting the basketball, don't just watch them shoot—crash the board and get positioned for the rebound. You may be smaller. You may be not as quick. But if you can get positioned, it gives you better access for the rebound.

In NASCAR, on the Saturday before a race, they have a trial to see who does laps the fastest. Then on Sunday, it gives them what's called the pole position—it determines where they start. If you get out in front, it helps you to avoid getting into a wreck early on. Everybody wants to be out in front, but many times, we feel like we are in the back.

Let me give you three tips for getting into position.

Ephesians 2:6 (NLT) says, "He raised us from the dead along with Christ and seated us with him in the heavenly realms because we are united with Christ Jesus." When we follow Jesus, we become a new creation, and in the spirit realm, we become seated with Him in the heavenly places. Therefore, if everything is under Jesus' feet, isn't it under our feet, too? Many times, believers say yes to Jesus and still have this victim mentality: that they're defeated, that they're just sinful failures who'll never be able to get it right. They don't ever shift in position. I've got to realize that, in Christ, I've gotten positioned to flourish. I've got to see myself like He does. We've got to shift our self-image because how you see yourself will determine what you experience in life.

King Saul was head and shoulders above everybody. He was the first king of Israel. And when Samuel came down to find Saul and present him as God's man of the hour, too sweet to be sour, God's tower of power—where was he? The Bible says he was hiding among the baggage. The reason Saul failed in his purpose, in the plans that God had for his life, is because he never saw himself like God did. Saul saw himself as from the weakest of the clan of Benjamin.

How many of us have the ability, the potential, the gifting for greatness, but we never make that clear in our own minds? How many of us sell ourselves short? If we see ourselves as little, we'll always be little. That's why we've got to look through the lens of Christ—to see ourselves like God does. Until we believe we are who God says we are, we can never do what He's called us to do. Saul could never rule as king because he didn't see himself that way. And I'm telling you, I've battled that. I remember when people first started calling me "pastor." I was like, "I'm not a pastor. Don't call me pastor." But then a lady said, "Pastor Michael, God is just trying to get you to see yourself as He sees you. You've got to embrace this title, this office, because that's what you're called to be. So just receive it, and stop rejecting it."

I've got to see myself as more than a conqueror. I've got to see myself as royalty because royalty destroys inferiority. When you step onto the stage, be comfortable. When you're nervous, it shows. When you're insecure, it shows. Just be comfortable. These great communicators and leaders—how can they get up in front of ten thousand people and feel so relaxed? It's because they've accepted who they are. It's not just competency and capacity, it's comfort. Be comfortable, knowing that you're a son, you're a daughter, you're gifted.

You've got to see yourself like God sees you. The enemy will tell you, "You have no heritage. You weren't raised in ministry. You're not worthy. You're not qualified. You've made too many mistakes. You don't have enough talent. You don't have the ability. You weren't trained enough. You didn't get the right education." But you can't think like that.

You've got to think, "I am positioned in Christ, and I am who God says I am. I am new. I'm forgiven." God says, "Get planted in My house, get positioned in Me, and I'm going to release favor. I'm going to break generational curses off your life. I'm going to restore blessing to your life and your children and your children's children, and I'll give you an inheritance." You are a joint-heir with Christ. You are favored. You are a new creation. You're God's child. You don't have to just sit at the back of the plane anymore because your dad owns the airline. Are you with me?

Isn't that what He said? "You're the top and not the bottom. You're above and not beneath. You're in front, not the back. You're the head, not the tail." I've got to get positioned in Christ. Position is everything.

Here's a second thing. *I've got to get positioned under His hand.* 1 Peter 5:6 (NIV) says, "Humble yourselves, therefore, under God's mighty hand that He may lift you up in due time." Dr. Jones used to say that all the time, and it really stuck with me. You don't have to lift yourself up. You don't have to promote yourself. God doesn't need our help getting us to the place where we flourish in life. We simply have to submit to Him, under His hand, and He will lift us up.

In the Hebrew culture of the Bible, fathers would lay hands on their children. You see this when Jacob stole the blessing from Esau. Isaac laid hands on Jacob and spoke a blessing. Esau was furious about it because they really believed that whatever the father said in those blessings was going to happen. Why doesn't this happen today? Because we don't believe it. But in the Jewish culture, this was a big thing. You see this in Genesis 48. Joseph had brought his family to him—the people of God—brought to Egypt to fulfill the purpose of God. Joseph had two sons. Jacob can barely see, so he said, "Bring your boys here. I want to release a father's blessing on their life."

Let's take a look at verses 12-15 and 17-20:

> So Joseph brought them from beside his knees, and he bowed down with his face to the earth. And Joseph took them both, Ephraim with his right hand toward Israel's left hand, and Manasseh with his left hand toward Israel's right hand, and brought them near him. Then Israel stretched out his right hand and laid it on Ephraim's head, who was the younger, and his left hand on Manasseh's head, guiding his hands knowingly, for Manasseh was the firstborn. . . . Now when Joseph saw that his father laid his right hand on the head of Ephraim, it displeased him, so he took hold of his father's hand to remove it from Ephraim's head to Manasseh's head. And Joseph said to his father, "Not so, my father, for this one is the firstborn; put your right hand on his head."

But his father refused and said, "I know, my son, I know.
He also shall become a people, and he also shall be great,
but truly his younger brother shall be greater than he, and
his descendants shall become a multitude of nations."
So he blessed them that day, saying, "By you Israel will
bless, saying, 'May God make you as Ephraim and as
Manasseh!'" And thus he set Ephraim before Manasseh.

Jacob's blessing brought an unexpected shift. And sometimes, we forget that we should have been under God's hand of judgment. But because of the cross, Jesus has crossed the hands, and now we get the blessing of God's mercy and favor as a child of God. But we've got to get under the hand. You need to know that God chose you, God knew you, and it's not by happenstance that He has put His hand upon your life.

What has this got to do with the people of God and the purpose of God? What does this have to do with the local church? At least in some part, we can find this in Ephesians 4:11 (NKJV): "And He Himself gave some to be apostles, some prophets, some evangelists, and some pastors and teachers." Jesus was going to heaven, and He left gifts for the church. You may not have realized this, but these are gifts for the church. It's the five-fold ministry gift. Jesus was all of these, but He tore them into five different pieces of Himself when He ascended and gave them back to the church. A great way to remember it is by using the fingers of your hand.

The first is the apostle: the thumb. The thumb is the strongest, so typically, apostles are pioneers. They're exemplified by a ram that is ramming a door open, breaking ground.

Then you've got your pointer finger: the prophet. Why? Prophets point the way.

Then you've got the middle finger. He reaches the farthest, so he's the evangelist.

Then you've got the ring finger, where we put a wedding band when we get married. This represents the pastor. He's married to the church. He's the shepherd. He cares for the flock, nourishing it, caring for it, serving it.

And then the pinky is the teacher. It brings balance, just like the teacher brings balance to the Word of God.

We need to get positioned under the hand. I need to come under spiritual authority.

We need to get positioned under the hand. I need to come under spiritual authority. I need to have these gifts speak into my life and lead me, encourage me, give me affirmation, equip me. But they also correct me. Many people get positioned in Christ, but they don't get under the hand because they think, *I don't need some leader. I've got Jesus.* We misunderstand scripture. We don't get positioned for favor. We don't grow, thrive, or flourish because we don't value the gift of God.

Jesus taught us a principle: "If you receive a prophet in the name of a prophet, you'll receive a prophet's reward." That's why it's so important for you to not talk about a pastor. I'm not talking about somebody who's had a moral failure, a financial failure, or something where they need to be removed and restored. I'm talking about somebody you don't like, some opinion you have about something they did that you didn't like. When you talk negatively about a pastor, you don't realize it, but now you've hindered somebody else's ability to receive the gift of God that's in them. Now, they see them after the flesh, and they don't see them as a divine gift of God.

So, even if you see weaknesses in my life, don't allow them to cause you to miss the gift and the anointing of God upon my life. Though you may have weaknesses in your flesh, don't disregard the gift and the anointing on your life. I've got to honor that gift. And if I receive that gift, I receive the gift on that gift in my life.

Jesus was a carpenter. When He went to His hometown, that's how they saw Him. Darius Daniels said, "You had the carpenter Jesus and you had the Christ Jesus. And how you perceived him determined which one you got." If you saw Him as a furniture maker, all He could give you was furniture. But that still didn't mean He wasn't the Christ. The Bible says He could not do any miracles in His hometown because of their unbelief. They didn't see Him as the Christ. They saw Him as Mary's son, Joseph's boy. In one town, He was the Messiah—miracles, signs and wonders—the dead brought to life, leprosy gone, blind eyes opened, fishes and loaves. In another town, He couldn't do anything but lay hands on a few sick people. That's why we have to learn how to honor ministry gifts.

The leadership gifts of Jesus represent the five-fold ministry gifts. And the Father speakers to you through pastors and leaders, evangelists, apostles and teachers. They help shape you. I'm not ignoring the fact that you have to be sent. You can't just get up and claim to have one of these gifts because it takes one to know one. There are guys out there who misuse the name. Others have valid gifts but are unhealthy—they've misused their authority to hurt people or manipulate them. Some of them have impure motives. But just like you can't throw away all doctors for a few bad ones, just like you can't throw away all policemen just because of a few of them, you can't throw out all pastors, apostles, evangelists, and teachers.

If we want to be blessed, we've got to recognize who is it that's been appointed in our lives. Who are the leaders you need to be under? In this generation, everybody wants to be the boss. In the kingdom of God, it's more important who you're under than who you're over. You inherit what you honor. Authority was never intended to harm you or control you, but to help you get to a place you could never get to on your own. I truly believe in my heart that I wouldn't be here today if I had not honored my pastors' authority in my life. It wasn't intended to harm me. It was intended to help me get to a place I never could have gotten to on my own.

Lastly, *I've got to get positioned in the Father's house* and stay planted like a tree so that I can be stable and fruitful and useful. So many people are pulling up their roots. And if you pull up a root too many times, it dies. That's not what God wants for your life. He wants you to get positioned in the Father's house and discover, develop, and deploy the greatness that's inside of you. Learn how to steward your time, your talents, and your treasures so that you can thrive. You may come to the Father's house broken like I was: lost, addicted, and wounded. But there were people there who loved me. And there were people in the Father's family who spoke life over me, believed in me, affirmed me, equipped me, and helped me a grow into what God had for me. I encountered His goodness and mercy.

I realized that precious promise that says, "Surely goodness and mercy will follow me all the days of my life." When I should have died, gone to prison, gotten the disease, or gotten killed, when I shouldn't have made it, that goodness and mercy followed me. They are promised when you're committed to the presence of God, the people of God, and the purpose of God.

You may have felt like you're at the back. You didn't get the breaks. You didn't come from the right family or have the right education. It's okay. When you learn how to honor God and His presence and the gifts in His house under His hand, He's going to move you to a new position, and you'll get to a place that you couldn't have reached because of your education, your talent, or the family you came from.

It's only by being in His presence, with His people, fulfilling His purpose, where He is most glorified and we are most satisfied. So get positioned in Christ, under His hand, in His house.

The biggest key to unlocking favor is staying planted. Staying in faith. Keeping your attitude in check. But also like I said earlier, it's how you see yourself. Activate your faith to speak things because our words have power. And a lot of times we're not using that. We don't really believe that our words have power. If we did, we'd be talking a lot every day. I'm not saying, "Hey, God, I want a Corvette." No, no, those are selfish ambitions. I'm talking about things that God's promised you in the Word. Your health, peace, protection, provision, the dream that God's given to you. Prophesying to it. Ezekiel spoke to the bones. I'm learning that positioning my mind is a big piece of it.

It's also your level of commitment. You get out of it what you put into it. I'm around high-level leaders, and they're just running at a different level. It's like the air's different up there, and you have to condition your lungs by being faithful and excellent with where you're at. I told Charla, "I feel like in the last two weeks God's been conditioning me." I used to could go to a conference and I'd be like, "Oh, is it over?" Now, it's like, "No, give me more." I'm going to shake that off. Give me more. I want to learn. I want to listen. Learn how to be faithful and expand your faith.

We miss a lot of favorable opportunities because we don't say yes to the right things. We're tired. We don't want to do *that*. But you don't know that that invitation might open the door for a connection, and you'll miss that. I know, through the years, I have. So our flesh can get us out of condition where we don't want to connect with people.

It could be God positioning us. You never know who the gatekeeper to your destiny is. That's why you can't live isolated and fulfill your destiny. It's going to take investment. It's going take relationships. Luke 2:52 (NIV) says, "And Jesus grew in wisdom and stature, and in favor with God and man." With God and man.

We were out in the conference area talking to pastors and a pastor's wife came, took me by the elbow, and said, "Pastor Ron wants you to come to the back. He wants to talk with you." Ron Carpenter. And so I go back to the green room, right, and I'm like wow. And so he gets on a s- sofa and he says this to me Milan. He says ah, "Now I don't really know what, you know, what all you're here for. Uh, I'm glad you're here. A, but I respect Dr. Sam Chand very much. And when Dr. Sam Chand tells me I need to get to know somebody, I pay attention to that. So, what can I do for you?

My point was Dr. Sam Chand made that happen. Ron Carpenter would have never done that.

So, that's why it's people. It's favor with people.

Six Degrees from Kevin Bacon.

being in the room with people, you catch things you can't unless you are in the room.

It wasn't about what was being taught- it was about what I needed to catch. Sam Chand, he texted me later. And he goes, "Hope I made a great connection today because we always need people who enlarge our world." And so being on a jet plane, that's what David Crank said. He said, " I felt like the Lord told me to invite you on this jet ride, jet journey- to expand your faith." And it did. So to me, it's being in position. So don't say no to connection. To opportunity.

CHAPTER 10

INTIMACY AND IMPACT

Psalm 84:1-4 (NLT) says:

How lovely is your dwelling place, O Lord of Heaven's armies.
I long, yes, I faint with longing to enter the courts of the Lord.
With my whole being, body and soul, I will shout joyfully to
the living God. Even the sparrow finds a home and the swallow
builds her nest and raises her young at a place near your altar O

Lord of Heaven's Armies, my King and my God. What joy for those who can live in your house, always singing your praises.

I love this psalm. It's a great one to meditate on. It's important to this book because there has been tension for decades around the idea of a church not being a building. We know that the people are the church, yet there's this belief out there that church buildings will never be filled again—that the church will never meet and congregate like it always has—that you don't have to have a building. Here's the thing: the house of God is the presence of God and the people of God.

We are the temple of the Holy Spirit when we come together. We are all living stones that make up a house. Each stone brings their faith, their gift, the presence of God, and it's a dwelling place. It's where God wants to dwell with His family. Inside of the house is typically a family. And you belong in God's family.

THE SONS OF KORAH

There are three Korahs in the Bible, but theologians believe that the sons of Korah who are credited with several psalms are actually tied to the Korah who rebelled against Moses and the people of God when they were in the wilderness. They decided to get their own leadership team, start their own church, and say, "Let's see who God's chosen here—us or you!" They went through all these supernatural signs that confirmed Moses as God's chosen leader for the people of Israel. And the earth opened up and swallowed Korah, his family, and the two other men behind Korah. Then fire came down from heaven.

Aren't you glad you live under grace? Do you see how casually we in the New Testament, especially in America, approach spiritual authority? It matters. Korah rebelled against the leadership, and it cost him his purpose, his calling. He didn't want to follow God. Moses was God's leader; when they rebelled against Moses, they were rebelling against God. When you bring your family to the house of God, you've got to realize that every decision that you make doesn't just affect you and your needs—it affects your family!

Korah made a poor decision. Fast-forward generations, and these descendants of Korah decided to go in a different direction. They decided to use their skill sets, abilities, and gifts to serve the leader God put over them. Now we read about them in the book of Psalms. Many of them were gatekeepers in David's house. Some of them were soldiers. One of them was a chief choir director. The sons of Korah were skilled musicians who also wrote. It didn't matter that their forefather didn't fulfill the will and the purpose of God—they chose to follow David and be a part of God's family in the earth and be in God's house. They used their skill set to go in a different direction.

The good news is it doesn't matter what your forefathers did. You can choose to use your gifts to glorify God and to come up under the loving leadership God wants you under so that He can grow the things out of you that He wants to grow out of you.

Jesus said, "Unless a grain of wheat dies it can never multiply" (John 12:24, author paraphrase). That's why we have to die to self to come up under leadership. Know that I'm not talking about a dominating, lording leadership. When Moses was rebelled against, he would get on his face, cry out to God, and beg God not to destroy the people. That's the kind of response we should have as leaders as well, quite frankly. Never take it personally when people resist your leadership or resist your direction—just know that it's probably not even you. Sometimes, it's God.

If you want to flourish in life, it matters whom you choose to align with for God's glory.

The sons of Korah rewrote their purpose. If you want to flourish in life, it matters whom you choose to align with for God's glory so that you can discover, develop, and deploy your personal greatness and rewrite your story. Perhaps your family tree will go in a direction that's God-honoring. What joy for those who live in God's house! They will continually be singing His praises. Being connected with God in His presence, with His people, living out His purpose, is true living, and it's the key to flourishing.

Maybe you're like I was: you don't have a long line of Christ-followers in your heritage. My mom took me to church as a child, and I went to church for a couple years but then went my own way. My dad did not serve the Lord, but that didn't disqualify me. I was a young twenty-something living recklessly, discouraged and defeated, a spiritual orphan who needed to belong and find my identity in the house of God. But the fact is that, before we come to Jesus, we're *all* spiritual orphans. That's why Jesus said, "I will not leave you nor forsake you" (Hebrews 13:5, ESV) and "I will not leave you orphans" (John 14:18, NIV). We can come to Christ through the Holy Spirit.

Look at what it says in Ephesians 2:18 (author paraphrase):

Now all of us can come to the Father through Christ by the way of the one Holy Spirit. And from now on you're not strangers and people who are not citizens. You are citizens together with those who belong to God.

Listen to me: you belong in God's family in God's house. When I came to the Father's house, I received His love, His grace, His mercy. I didn't realize God wanted to simply make me a part of His family. Look at Romans 8:29 (NLT): "For God knew His people in advance. And He chose them to become like His Son so that His Son would be the first-born among many brothers and sisters." I want you to think about this: Jesus is our Savior, but He's also the firstborn among the brothers and sisters. Let me say it like this: Jesus is not the only Son of God anymore. He's the *divine* Son of God. But now we, because of Christ, are sons and daughters. We are joint-heirs with Jesus. If He's royal, guess what? We are! We're royal. So we must also, like Jesus, be about the Father's business. We are not to be saved and believe on Jesus and go our merry way. We are not to buy into a philosophy that says, "I say yes to Jesus, and now it's this personal, private thing." That's not biblical. That's not the Father's way. That's not the kingdom way. You were saved for a purpose. It's all about discovering your identity.

Faith can conquer a giant, but until you know your identity, you can never fulfill your destiny. God wants you to know who you are and whose you are because then you'll know what you can do. Jesus didn't do a single miracle before Matthew 3. He was thirty years old, which by the way, in the Jewish culture, is the sign of maturity. You can't even be a rabbi until you're thirty, and you must have studied your whole life. When Jesus was baptized, the Spirit of the Lord descended upon Him and a voice from heaven in Matthew 3:17 (author paraphrase) said, "This is my son. In Him, I am well pleased." When He heard His Father's voice, that human side of Jesus was affirmed, and He knew who He was. Before He did anything for His Father, the Father was already pleased with Him. He knew who He was, and so He knew what He could do. He went into the wilderness, He was tested by the enemy, and He came out in power—that's where the supernatural signs and wonders came from. When you know who you are, you'll know what you can do.

When you doubt yourself and what God can do through you, you've lost the sense and the focus of your identity. That's why it's important for us to understand our identity as God's sons and daughters. We've become a part of God's family. And it's in God's house, the dwelling place of *Yahweh*, that we can fulfill God's plan.

This is not just something that religion came up with. Some people who seem knowledgeable and educated will tell you that religion started with Catholicism. Did the Catholics take religion and use it to control? Absolutely. Did the devil get in there and mess up what God was doing? Yeah. You know, the Christian movement was actually turned into Roman Catholicism because the Christians overtook the world, and the leaders of Rome said, "We've got to get in on this. They've turned the world upside down." Then they stopped letting people read the Bible. My point is that we can't let some fragmented, twisted, perverted experience define God's Word. It's God's house, and the first house that we see is in the Garden of Eden. It was paradise. God created Adam, and then He created Eve.

In fact, if I could talk about it for a second, when He saw that Adam was made in His image, and said in Genesis 2:18 (author paraphrase), "It's not good that he is alone," what He was saying was, "It's not good that he is alone or *all one*." So, He went to the dirt one time, created Adam, and then reached inside of Adam and took Eve out. Their coming together was God's idea. They were in the garden, in the tabernacle, in the dwelling place of *Yahweh*. And then we see that God gave them the great assignment: take dominion. "Be fruitful and multiply." This is my desire: to reproduce my family, in my house, with my children. God wants a family. It's always been His desire, and God's going to have what He wants. So I want to make sure that I'm coming into agreement with the Father.

To be fruitful and multiply means God is actually saying, "Stay connected to me, and reproduce my image in the earth." John 15 tells us that if we abide in Christ, we'll bear much fruit. That's why we say discipleship is transmitting a way of thinking; we are image-bearers of *Yahweh*—not just physically, but spiritually. Legacy isn't just something you build; it's someone you raise up. That's why we have to be committed to passing on our faith to the next generation. We have to teach them to value church. When I get in church on Sunday, and I see a lot of gray hair, I get concerned. We don't want ours to be a personality-driven ministry that's over after I pass the baton. Whom am I reaching out to that's a generation down? What children can you invite to church? Maybe you've never done that. Get outside of your comfort zone!

Satan despised that Adam and Eve were in communion with God. He despised the fact that God loved them without condition and wanted to multiply them in the earth. His whole goal was to slander God, to get them to question what God said. Isn't that true today? Maybe you've shared your faith with people and invited them to church. What do they typically criticize first? The Bible. "Can we really trust it? Wasn't it written by men?" You know who that is? That's the devil, still trying to slander and question the Word of God. It's what he did to Eve, and it's what got them into trouble.

Maybe there's a narrative in your mind that's convincing you that it's time to leave the church. If that's the case, you really need to get some accountability, and put that thought before some people, put it before the Lord. The enemy is a master of creating narratives to get you to believe a lie. It could be that he's trying to get you out of position, just like he did Adam and Eve. The work of the enemy is to get people out of God's dwelling place, doing their own thing. It doesn't matter if it's a "good thing." It could be out on a Little League baseball field. It could be at the lake with the family. People think, *We're just having family time. I'm not sacrificing my family for some church.* No one's ever asked you to. But you also don't sacrifice your purpose in the family of God for your family of origin.

If I was just trying to build some organization, I'd go build something else because this is the toughest organization you'll ever try to build. I could go out and be shrewd in the corporate world and just do what needs to be done, but that's not us. We're not of the world. We serve with our authority, and we love people. We want people to win. We want to pastor people. We lay down our life for the sheep because we're shepherds, not hirelings.

See, hirelings, when the wolf comes, run. But shepherds lay down their lives. They take the hits. They show the grace. They show the patience. They show the love. They give the forgiveness. They keep believing. The enemy even took one third of the angels out of the place of God's presence. He's still trying to do it now. And we've gotta realize that our enemy isn't people, while still pulling down strongholds in people's thinking with truth.

It's not about you being a great doer. God is the great I Am, not the Great Doer. God's more interested in who you're becoming than what you're doing. In fact, who you're becoming will cause the good things He wants done to spring out of you. Passion for God's family is God's answer to loneliness. All of us are born into a family of origin, just like the sons of Korah. We didn't choose it—we're born a spiritual orphan, we're far from God, dead in our sins. But God's desire is that none perish and that we have a knowledge of Christ—that's why He sent Jesus.

Listen to Ephesians 1 and 9 (author paraphrase): "God decided in advance to adopt us into His own family by bringing us to Himself through Jesus Christ. . . . This is what He wanted to do, and it gave

Him great pleasure." You're not here today just because you chose to be good and start following Jesus. He chose you and brought you to Himself. He opened your eyes through His spirit and revealed Christ to you so that you could be born again. There are only two ways to get into a family: being born and being adopted. God does both for us. We're born again by the Spirit, and then we're adopted by the blood of Jesus.

In Roman law, if you're an adopted son, you have just as much right to the inheritance as a natural-born child. That's important. God's family is the church of the living God, the pillar and the foundation of the truth. So this means that the church isn't something you go to; it's something that you *are*. It's something you belong to. Through Jesus we've become children of God. We have access as children now to the family of God, the dwelling place of *Yahweh*, God's house, which means we shouldn't be timid or slow to take advantage of that access.

I love my children. They know they have access to me anytime. They'll walk into my office—I've got to teach them to knock—but they're sons and daughters with unlimited, all-access passes. So don't be timid, don't be shy, don't be lacking in faith. Believe big.

My place in God's family offers me intimacy, but it's my function that offers me impact.

You have access to the Father, to His presence, to His provision, to His purpose. We have a function. My place in God's family offers me intimacy, but it's my function that offers me impact. So not only does God want intimacy with me—He wants impact through me. There's intimacy, there's transformation, that happens in me with Him. Some of us get stuck here. If we're not careful, we become consumers of worship. Arenas are filling up with some incredible worship teams. And it's great that people are going to worship Jesus—that's better than the club. But if they don't leave that place and go make an impact, what was it for? What is our church for if we've got the best worship and the best preaching, but the people don't leave and make an impact? Yes, we are saved by grace, but we're saved to do good works. We have a function.

I've been married for twenty-four years this coming April. When Charla said yes to me, I was positioned as her husband, and that gave me great benefits. She's my best friend. We laugh, we have fun, we have life together. We have romance. It's awesome. My place gives me access to benefits, but that doesn't express my love for her. That's my function as a husband—to love her as Christ loves the church. To serve her, wash her with the water of the Word, affirm her, care for her, pastor her, provide for her, and protect her.

So it's not my *place* that shows my love; it's my *function*. If she's not feeling the love, I can't say, "Hey babe, I'm going to enjoy some benefits and then I'm going to go fishing and golfing with the guys for about a week. If I want some more benefits, I'll see you then." How many of you know our marriage is not going to last if that's my approach?

It's the same way in our family. As a Turner child, you have access, but you also have a function. If you ask my children, "What says I love you to Dad?" they'll tell you, "When we do what he asks us. When we serve, take care of the house, when we function as a member of the house—that's how you show Dad some love." If Dad comes home and the trash is overflowing and the dishes are dirty and there's poop on the floor and the beds are not made, that does not say "I love you" to Dad.

So as a child of God, know that you have intimacy, but you also have function. And it's intimacy that transforms you. You'll always be a child of God, but it's for impact. We don't get to just enjoy intimacy until we get to heaven. God doesn't need your good works, but earth does because God wants His family to be fuller, and He's commissioned us as sons and daughters to go make it happen.

Before you can walk in your purpose, you've got to be planted in God's house, with God's presence, God's people, and God's purpose, where He wants you. Find a local church that you love, and get planted. That's my true desire for you.

I also want you to understand how important it is that you have that conviction. You shouldn't be ashamed or fearful about talking to somebody about serving on your team. You've got to say, "I'm a son of God. I have access and intimacy. They are children of God. They may not know their function and that God has a purpose for them, but it's actually how they fulfill the purpose and the plan of God for their life, and it's actually how they are fulfilled the most!" When you're serving other people, and your eyes aren't on just you, it actually causes you to rise up to a higher level. And what you make happen for others, God makes happen for you. If you're sitting around just waiting for God to do it all, that's not a great plan. So receive and give. And even when you're not feeling it, keep giving. Isn't that the greatest act of faith, by the way? That's why we say act your way into a feeling.

Sometimes, I don't feel like giving financially. But it doesn't matter if I feel it. If God led me to do it, I've got to lead myself into that action by faith. Then, after I give, guess what I have? A lot of joy. We've got to help people find their function. Every person has a function. When you're born again, and you realize who you are, there's something inside of you that says, *I've got to do something for Him. I want to give my all.*

Remember Psalm 92, which mentions the palm tree and the cedars of Lebanon? Cedars were a sign of wealth. They were considered a gift to the people of Lebanon. They were strong, thick, and highly desired. They had a pleasing aroma that was also able to drive away insects. Solomon's temple was actually built with the cedars of Lebanon. So we see that God says that, "If you're planted in My house, you're going to be durable. You're going to be stable."

How about the palm tree? The palm tree in Scripture is always the date palm. It's beautiful. It has a deep taproot called a root ball, and it can flourish in a desert. Have you ever seen a palm tree in a desert where there's no water? Isn't that amazing? Even in a dry land, that palm tree can still flourish. God says, "That's what you're like. Even when you go through the wilderness, you can still be plush and green." It also produced dates, which give way to sugar, wine, honey, oil, resin, rope, tannin, and dye. Its seeds were fed to cattle. The leaves were used for roofs, fences, mats, and baskets. Think about that. God says, "When you're planted in My house, you're going to be like a cedar—durable and stable. You're going to be like a palm tree—fruitful, and you're going to be useful."

Here's the other cool thing about palm trees: have you ever seen a palm tree in a hurricane? It can endure gale force winds. In a storm, oak trees are going to break. Pine trees are going to snap. But that palm tree bends. And scientists say that, after the storm is over, it's actually stronger and even grows! When you're planted in the house of the Lord—when the storms of life hit your life—you may bend, but you're not going to break. You're going to bow down and worship in the middle of the storm, and when the storm is over, you're still going to be planted, stronger than ever.

Hebrews 10:24-25 (NLT) says,

> *Let us think of ways to motivate one another to acts of love*
> *and good works. Let us not neglect our meeting together,*
> *as some people do, but encourage one another, especially*
> *now as the day of His return is drawing near.*

Our function is acts of love. Let's think of ways to motivate people to get on our ministry teams. Let us think of ways to motivate people to good works. Let us think of ways for people to find their function. It's gathering. When we understand the function, especially as the day of

His return is nearer than ever, we'll have a passion to reach people, to pastor people, to disciple people, and to mobilize people.

Everything I need is in the Father's house. Your place gives you intimacy, but your function gives you impact to expand God's kingdom and enlarge His family in the earth. It's not about you being perfect; it's about you shining and being an image-bearer of Jesus, as a child of God—displaying your function through good works that bring glory and honor to His name.

To be fruitful and to multiply means to be planted in God's house so that you can flourish in life—it's the place where God is most glorified, and you are most satisfied.

CHAPTER 11

WE WILL ROCK YOU

'Ve been an Atlanta Braves fan since I can remember. They won a World Series in 1995. There have been years of hopeful titles, but only one actually happened. In 2021, they once again had an opportunity to bring some honor back to Atlanta. They were underdogs and counted out all year due to injuries, but they prevailed. In sports, a lot of times, there is not just competition but a lot of trash talk. I played sports in high school, but I was never a trash-talker. I just let my game do the talking.

There's this other champion who was a trash talker. In 1 Samuel 17, we read that his name was Goliath. This story might not be familiar to you, but Goliath was a giant. They believe he was upwards of nine feet tall. For forty days and forty nights, he taunted the promises of God and the people of God:

> *He stood and shouted a taunt across to the Israelites. "Why are you all coming out to fight? I'm the Philistine champion, but you're only the servants of Saul. Choose one man to come down here and fight me, and if he kills me then we'll be your slaves. But if I kill him, you will be ours. I defy the armies of Israel today." —1 Samuel 18:8-9 (NLT)*

As Goliath was defying the people of God, he was also defying the God of the people.

Verse 11(NLT) says, "When Saul and the Israelites heard this, they were terrified and deeply shaken." Goliath knew he had the advantage, but now he'd brought God into his taunt, which is never a good idea. For forty days and forty nights, the Israelites were terrified because they were listening to the wrong voice. Even today, those who call upon the name of the Lord can find ourselves in seasons where they are listening to the wrong voices: those that intimidate us, point out our weaknesses, cause us to doubt ourselves, to doubt God. These giants cause inferiority and insecurity: "You'll never beat the addiction. You'll never get over the pain. You'll never have God's best for your life. Your kids will never serve God. You'll never have kids. You'll never be married. People will never value your gift." We can become paralyzed, shaken, and afraid. Our challenges can be so in-our-face that we get our eyes on the problem and off of the promise.

Enter a young man named David, who was really an underdog. I think I identify with David in that sense—I've felt like an underdog a time or two. David realized who he was, so he realized what he could do. God is trying to get you to remember your past is gone, you're a born-again child of God, and when He sees you, He sees Jesus, in whom He is "well pleased." Know that your Father already approves of you and is pleased with you before you do anything.

David stepped up. He had stopped listening to the wrong voice. It reminds me of a story I heard Zig Ziglar tell about a young man who was in a small town:

The boy didn't have a father and had been raised by his mom. In fact, it was kind of the talk of the town: "Who is his father? Do we know who she was with? I wonder what his dad is like? I wonder who his dad is?" The boy felt this pressure from the other children, and even other families, and he would walk around town and get looked at. He knew there was this looming perception that he was unwanted by his father. So he decided to go to church one night, and the pastor said, "If you're new here, I want you to stand up. I want you to meet me at the back. I want to shake everybody's hand." So the pastor went back and was shaking hands, and he came up to little Ben and said, "Where's your father, son? Who's your dad?" And the little boy, Ben, just put his head down because he didn't have the courage to say, "I don't know."

And then the pastor said, "Hold on, wait a second. I know who your daddy is. I see the family resemblance. Your father is God." That little boy picked his head up with a tear in his eye, and from that moment, little Ben Hooper said, "I realized who I was that day."

Well, little Ben Hooper went on to become a governor in the state of Arkansas. Don't ever forget the voice of your Father affirming who you are. Even if your mother and your father forsake you, your everlasting Father never will. He formed you; He's for you, in you, and with you. He will never leave you, and He believes in you. When you believe that, you, too, can start listening to the right voice and do great things.

Ephesians 2:10 (NLT) says, "We are God's masterpiece, created anew in Christ Jesus, so we can do the good things He planned for us long ago." Before God ever created you, He already created great things for you to do in life. You have a purpose, but most people never discover it, and they go to their grave never having deployed their greatness for the glory of God in the earth.

When God created you, He gave you this little thing on your finger: a fingerprint. Typically, if people want to know something about you, they go to your fingerprint—it's usually for a negative reason. They're looking for somebody who did something bad. But in God's kingdom, your fingerprint isn't used to identify something bad that you did—it's used to help you identify something great you can do through the glory and the grace of God. It's a unique thing.

No one in history has ever had your fingerprint. No one in the future will ever have your fingerprint. It's the one thing that separates you from every other person who's ever breathed oxygen on planet Earth. Think about that. One report said that babies have smooth skin in their mother's womb, and that it's through the pressures of the womb that they form little wrinkles that give them their unique fingerprints.[6] It just reminds me that, in life, when we go through challenges and struggles, they're not meant to take us out. They're meant to cause us to be unique and to step into our greatness.

> **When we go through challenges and struggles, they're not meant to take us out. They're meant to cause us to be unique and to step into our greatness.**

You see, butterflies aren't made just because somebody waved a wand. They go into a cocoon where it's tight, and over time and with pressure, they come out butterflies. A piece of coal goes under pressure before it becomes a diamond. So don't get upset about the pressure; just know that God is forming you and the good things that are inside of you that are going to come forth.

---

6 Stephanie Watson, "How Fingerprinting Works," 24 March 2008, *HowStuffWorks,* https://science.howstuffworks.com/fingerprinting.htm.

So you have a fingerprint. It's the 1-percent difference. In fact, 99 percent of all human DNA is the same. That's why you can have an Asian man give an African American man his heart. You can have a Hispanic lady give an Indian woman a kidney. That's why we can't get caught up by the hue of our skin. We all bleed the same color, and we're all saved by the same color. The same blood that saved you saved me. It's not about the outer man; it's about the inner man. But there's a 1-percent difference in us. Could it be that that's the unique, divine glory that God has put inside of each one of us? It's the fingerprints no one else has. You can leave a mark no one else can. Will you leave your fingerprint in this life for the glory of God?

It's time to stop hiding from the giants. You don't have to be perfect to be used by God; you just have to be available. David stepped into who God said he was. He'd already been anointed as king, yet he had not taken his position. He was actually overlooked by his father. Some believe that he was the son of a mistress that his father never married. He was the youngest of eight, and he was probably chosen to be the shepherd because nobody wanted to get out there with stinky sheep. But we see that he served his father with honor, faithfully, which just reminds us that God doesn't need our help to get us to our place of promotion and destiny. In fact, Psalm 75:6 says promotion doesn't come from the north, south, east, or the west. Promotion comes from the LORD, so stop being envious, and stop trying to jockey. Stop being frustrated. Stop beating yourself up, and just rest. Become the best version of yourself, and know that, in due season, God is going to elevate you and promote you. When you humble yourself, He's going to lift you up. The pressure is off. God's got this.

You're called to make a difference in your family, in your church, in your school, in culture, for the glory of God. You're called to break the chain of addiction, to break generational iniquities, and to establish a legacy in the earth for the glory of God. You are called to be fruitful and to multiply for the glory of God. You are called to stay connected to God and reproduce His image in the earth. You have a high calling.

This giant was taunting, but David was willing to take a risk and be bold. In that moment, he knew that his Father in heaven had already anointed Him and said, "You're royalty. Your earthly father may have overlooked you, but make no mistake, I've heard your prayers. I've seen your faithfulness serving those sheep when nobody else wanted to. I've seen your faithfulness when you were willing to face a lion because you knew how valuable the sheep were to your father. You were willing to face a bear just because you knew that little sheep had value to your earthly father. I see you, David." David stepped up in this authority and confidence. He wasn't perfect, but he was available.

He said in 1 Samuel 17:29 (NKJV): "Is there not a cause?" David looked at the people of God terrified by the giant of the day, silenced and sidelined. There is a spirit of Goliath loose in the land today that is taunting the church, trying to get the church to be sidelined and silenced. But let's make a declaration today that no giant is going to sideline God's people! We are going to live boldly, audaciously—with humility. Make no mistake about it; we're not going to be afraid. "Is there not a cause?" Is there not a cause for the local church? At Turning Point, there is a reason God launched us on the south side of Atlanta. There is a reason He's called us to be a multicultural, multigenerational, multi-site, multimillion dollar debt-free distribution center in the earth for the glory of god. There is a cause.

Saul tried to give David his armor and his sword, but it didn't fit. It wasn't tested; it wasn't proven. Saul could use it in his calling and in his generation, but David had to use what God called him to use. That's why you can't be envious of somebody else's gift because God's given you an amazing gift. God will never help you be somebody else, but He'll always help you to become the best version of yourself. You just need to realize you have a fingerprint that nobody else has and nobody else will have, and you can leave a mark that nobody else can.

David stooped down and got five stones. Five is the number of grace. We're going to see that David only needed one. Why did he get five? Some believe Goliath had four brothers, and David thought, *I've got one for every one of you.* He knew who he was, and he knew what he could do. We see that this stone was his uniqueness. No one had ever brought a sling and a rock to a sword and a spear fight, but the sling and the stone were part of David's uniqueness. That's why we can't shut down the next generation and the way that they want to approach the kingdom of God. God will give us a stone and a rock for every generation, and what worked in Grandma's generation isn't going to work today. That's why we want to be a culture that's multigenerational. We don't want this thing to end with us. There are plenty of churches who focused on one generation, and today, they're empty facilities. That's why we've got to continue to reach children. We want this thing to be generational. God is the god of Abraham, Isaac, and Jacob.

David has to use the thing that he's tested. It was his X factor. Could it be that you have a rock that represents your fingerprint? "How do I identify it?" you may ask. Let me just give you three thoughts. This is something that I feel like God's put me on the earth to do: to help you identify your rock so that you can sling it for the glory of God in your generation. There are giants that need to fall, and God is looking for some Davids.

Number one is this: *discover your purpose.* According to a 2009 Barna study, "Nearly two-thirds of the self-identified Christian population who claim to have heard about spiritual gifts have not been able to accurately apply whatever they have heard or what the Bible teaches on the subject to their lives."[7] How can you fulfill your purpose if you don't know why you were made? It's very simple. Rick Warren said it best in *The Purpose Driven Life*, the second-best seller of all time right under the Bible:

It's the age old question. What on Earth am I here for? Isn't there more? And at the bottom level, as simple as it gets, it's this. You were made by God and you were made for God. You were made to love God and to love others. You were created to know Him and to make Him known.[8]

The church in the New Testament understood this. The reason they met in the temple every day for prayer and for fellowship, for communion— the reason they were so committed to the glory of God, that people were getting added to the church weekly and miracles were happening—is

---

7 "Survey Describes the Spiritual Gifts That Christians Say They Have," *Barna Group*, 9 Feb. 2009, https://www.barna.com/research/survey-describes-the-spiritual-gifts-that-christians-say-they-have/.

8 Rick Warren, *The Purpose Driven Life*, (Grand Rapids: Zondervan, 2002).

because they realized that it was the only thing that mattered for the rest of their lives.

As Christ-followers, we've got to have a passion for what God's passionate about. To love Jesus means to love the things He loves and hate the things He hates. It's not, "Hey, Jesus, I've got a dream. Come on, tag along." No, it's, "Jesus, what is the dream that You have for my life? Because I have been bought with a price. My life is not my own. It's not about selfish ambition. It's about a sanctified ambition to know You and to make You known."

When I discovered my purpose, I discovered my passion. I was always a pretty passionate person. I liked to compete in sports. I loved music. I liked to dance a little. But my passion was misplaced. A lot of us have misplaced our passion. I was talking with one of our interns. We were talking about the Braves. He drives down to see them play. He said, "You know, pastor. I got convicted. I realized something: I can be more passionate about the Braves winning than I am about my church winning."

It's easy, even as Christ-followers, to misplace our passion. You could be more passionate about horses. You could be more passionate about Little League baseball. But I'm not going to walk into the house of God and give Jesus less than I give to somebody who hit a baseball. I'm not going to be more passionate about some other place than I am about the house of God. In fact, the house of God is a perfect place to invest your passion. David said Psalm 69:9 (author paraphrase), "Passion for your house consumes me." Jesus' passion was described in John 2:17 (author paraphrase), "Zeal for your house consumes me." And if I pattern my life after King David and Jesus, I think that's a life well-lived. I'm not saying you can't like those other things. I'm just saying you can't be more passionate about them than you are for God and for the kingdom of God.

As we commit to knowing Him, get in a personal relationship with Him, learn how to read the Bible and pray, as we worship and walk with Him, we discover our purpose. That's why we have a discovery process at Turning Point where you can even take a spiritual gifts test. It's not a science. It's simply a journey to begin to discover how God wired you. Because your wiring actually leads to your destiny. And your passion will come through as you commit to discovering your purpose. As you commit to serving God and serving people, your purpose will become more evident to you. And you take it step by step.

Then you begin to answer the passion question: what moves you to tears? When we started Turning Point, the reason we chose Henry County was because it bothered me that it was the sixth-fastest-growing county in the nation, and 85 percent of the people were not in a local church. Eighty-five percent of Henry Countians were not experiencing the house of God like I was. I realized that they were missing out on what God could do in their lives—in their purposes. When I first got saved, I remember I was passionate for teenagers. I still am. But that kind of evolved when I became a dad, and I became passionate about dads. Now, I'm turning this corner. I'm fifty-one, and my kids are coming into the young adult phase. I've got this passion for raising up legacy-minded men who understand their purpose, their call, and their authority, and women who understand their place in the kingdom of God who are going to establish God's legacy in the earth for His glory.

Charla's got a passion too: fighting against human trafficking. It's a part of her purpose. A part of your purpose is to solve a problem, to bring *shalom* to chaos. She has a passion for abused women and for protecting babies from being aborted. And she will go to war with the enemy over that. She'll fight a giant over that.

Our passion is the fuel that will cause us to speak to giants. When the giant taunted David in 1 Samuel 17:43 (author paraphrase), "Am I a dog that you're bringing a sling and a stone?" David responded in verse 45, "You come at me with a spear and a sword. But I come at you in the name of the LORD." Passion will cause you to charge a nine-foot giant with a rock in your hand. Passion will fuel you. David said in verse 36, "I killed the lion, and I killed the bear. I can kill this giant too." He was recounting the faithfulness of God. A giant may be taunting you, but just remember: He's done it before, and He's going to do it again.

Secondly, *you've got to develop your vision*. This isn't just what you see out there but what's inside of you, too.

David's predecessor, Saul, was head and shoulders above everybody. He was chosen and anointed. But he was insecure. He wanted to please the people and not God, and it cost him his calling. In fact, Samuel said 1 Samuel 15:17 (author paraphrase), "You've got to stop seeing yourself as small. You're the king." Some of us can step into a place of authority and calling, but if we don't believe what God says about us, we can never do the things He says He wants to do through us. I've got to develop my vision.

That's why I recommend that every day you have confessions. There's power in your confession. There's power in your words— life and death. The Bible says faith comes by hearing, and hearing by the Word of God. When I speak the Word of God to myself, guess what happens? Faith arises. This morning, I was walking my dog. Here was my confession: "The Spirit of the LORD is upon me because He has anointed me to preach the good news. He's anointed me to set captives free. He has anointed me to bring deliverance. He has anointed me to declare the year of God's favor. He has anointed me to heal the brokenhearted." That's my version of Luke 4:18-19. What I am doing? I am building faith in myself so that, when I show up in front of you, I've got faith.

So I've got to develop the vision because if I look at myself, I start seeing my weaknesses, my frailties, my shortcomings. I've got this inner critic. Maybe you have one, too. I'm having to constantly come against that inner critic because he's trying to pitch a narrative that's not really who I am. I've got to develop my vision of who God says I am, and I've got to take a stance against the wrong voice and start listening to the right voice. That way, I can step into who God has called me to be. And that's when I can stand before the giant and sling my rock.

You've got to stop looking back and realize that what's in front of you is greater than what's behind you.

You've also got to develop your vision of what God can do through your life. You've got to stop looking back and realize that what's in front of you is greater than what's behind you. That's why your rearview mirror is smaller than your front windshield. If you live in the back of your mind thinking about what they did to you or didn't do to you or didn't do for you—if you think about where you missed it and made it—you're going to miss out on what's possible.

You've got to develop a vision of what God says you can do. You can kill this giant. You can fulfill your calling. You can have that marriage and family. You can start that business, write that book, lose the weight, beat that disease, and reverse that inequity and that curse. You can be pulled into your future by the vision.

Whatever God's called you to do, it is connected to the house of God. You may go into the medical field, but when you go into the medical field, Jesus said, "Occupy 'til I come." You're not like the other doctors; you're bringing the kingdom of God, laying on of hands, faith. You're praying for patients, you're sharing Jesus. If you're a coach, it's the same thing. Yeah, you want to get the win, but if your kids go to hell, did you really win? As a business owner, you may win the world and have an incredible corporation, but if your children go to hell, did you really win? That's why I say things like, "Find a local church that you love, and get connected." We live in a consumer culture, but when it comes to the house of God, you're not a consumer; you're a contributor. Yes, you can consume, but the greatest level in God is not consuming, it's contributing.

When the vision is clear, results appear. You've got to see yourself like God. Begin to discover your gifts. Discover it, develop it, and here's the last one. *You've got to deploy your gifts.* You've must take action. Here's what I know: you'll never be perfect, and conditions will never be perfect.

But now is the perfect time. That's why the Bible says, "Now, is the day of salvation." Stop putting it off. Today is the day.

David ran at this giant, he slung his rock, and he killed that giant. He deployed the rock. There's greatness inside of you. Stop listening to the wrong voices. Stop waiting for conditions to be perfect to start serving God, to make a difference in the local church. Jesus said, "Take up your cross and deny yourself." People would come up to Jesus and say, "Jesus I want to follow you, but I have to go bury my dad first."

Jesus said, "Let the dead bury the dead. You come right now." Jesus always calls out our excuses.

Now is the time. The world needs you. Don't die without releasing your fingerprint. Don't leave this earth without discovering, developing, and deploying the greatness Jesus put inside of you before you even got your name. There are people you can reach. People you can serve. People you can impact. People you have a compassion for that others don't. God is saying, "I need you to step in and step out. Deploy that rock." It starts by serving. David was serving the sheep. David served his father. David killed a bear, and eventually, in one day, he killed a giant. He went from the pasture to the palace. He became the king's son-in-law. He deployed his greatness. And I think it's time for God's people to pick up their rock and deploy it.

Maybe you've been listening to the wrong voices. Maybe you've been sidelined or overlooked like David. Maybe you've been waiting for perfect conditions or thought you had to be perfect. But what would happen if you took a step of faith today? Go ahead, pick up a rock, and make a declaration that you're going to discover, develop, and deploy your fingerprint, the rock that God has given to you—that you're going to throw it at the giant in your generation. This giant must fall, but it can't fall until you deploy what God's put in your hand.

Maybe you need to be the husband God's called you to be, to lead your wife, to lead your family. Maybe you need to get over what happened in a previous relationship. Stop talking about what they did, and how you can't get involved, and how you can't trust people because people hurt you. We get hurt through people, but watch this, we also get healed through people. And the enemy wants you to focus on the hurt because he's trying to keep you from the healing. Maybe it's an addiction. Maybe it's time to step up and start serving God. Maybe God's called you to mentor teenagers, or children. Maybe God's called you to get a part of your local church ministry.

I don't know what He's calling you to do, but it's time to discover, develop, and deploy your rock.

CHAPTER 12

SUCCESS STARTS ON SUNDAY

As we conclude our journey through the principles of flourishing in life by being planted in the house of God, I think it's important to make clear that God does want us to thrive and succeed in life, marriage, family, and purpose, but God's version of success is different from culture's. The world says, "Grind, hustle, want it all, have it all, get it all you can, sleep when you're dead, and succeed at whatever cost."

We see the results: unhealthy lives, families, marriages, and mental and physical health. These are the prices most pay for success. Many are checking out, burning out, and wrecking the things that they say matter the most. When asked, "How are you doing?" most say, "Great . . . busy!" All important people are busy, right? But busyness doesn't equal importance, productivity, or meaning.

Have you ever noticed that many people answer the question of how they are with, "Tired"? We are living in a generation of fatigue. Most people live busy, unfulfilled, exhausted, and stressed. We can be led to believe that, if we only had more time . . . we could accomplish everything. But the truth is that if we had more time, we would probably fill it with something that doesn't replenish us but depletes us even more. If you got an unexpected day off, chances are you wouldn't spend hours in the presence of God but on errands, bills, honey-do lists, work, or emails. The urgent overwhelms us.

Busyness and striving can pull us off healthy rhythms and leave us more exhausted and burnt out. We can't do it all and have it all. We have the power to choose how we invest our time and lives. So many want to know how to balance their lives. The Bible doesn't teach a principle of balance but of order. Order determines capacity. When I get the order right, or put the big rocks in the container of my days, I will find that I can still have space to do other things that are less important and actually enjoy them.

Ephesians 5:15-17 (NLT) says, "So be careful how you live. Don't live like fools, but like those who are wise. Make the most of every opportunity in these evil days. Don't act thoughtlessly, but understand what the LORD wants you to do." Be careful, or the lure of other things will drag you away from the things that you say matter most. You'll find yourself in a marginless and meaningless lifestyle. It is not even an issue of wrong or right but an issue of limited time. Life is a vapor. Every day is a gift. Is it WISE to invest our time in (fill in the blank) when measured eternally?

How do we schedule wisely? We learn to have the faith and courage to say no to good things so that we can yes to the best things. When we say yes to one thing, we ultimately say no to something else. So be careful how you live. Know what the will of the Lord is for your life. We burn the candle at both ends and end up burning out. Did you know that our loving, wise God and Father has given us the remedy for burn out? It is called the Sabbath.

In Scripture, this is the only day that God set apart. It's the only one that has a name. It's actually so important that it's one of the Ten Commandments. *Sabbath* means to cease from your normal work and routine and to rest. We should not live to work. We should not be chained to a daily grind without end. The sabbath principle unchains us weekly. Sabbath is meant to be a day of peace—a day where we don't try to produce and conquer the world. We stop and rest in it. We live in an anti-sabbath culture, where we want to have two jobs with a side hustle and be a day trader. We want to be involved in everything for fear of missing out.

When it comes to the order of our time, days, and lives, I believe God is to be first.

God is a God of order. Order precedes blessings. Order determines capacity. I can control the controllable and leave the uncontrollable to God. When it comes to the order of our time, days, and lives, I believe God is to be first: first in our day, first in our relationships, first in our finances. Jesus rose on the first day of the week, which is a main reason why we as believers worship in community on Sunday. I believe that success for our week starts on Sunday, where we cease from our normal work to worship, serve, give, and connect as family of choice in the local church. Yes, we can do it any day and every day, but we should honor a sabbath-day principle.

Founder and owner of Chick-fil-A, Truett Cathy, believed this so strongly that he decided, when they launched, his business would not be open so that He and his employees could honor God with a sabbath in a local church of their choice. That business decision seems to have worked pretty well. They do billions in revenue now. They could have sold a lot of Chick-fil-A on a Sunday to people but decided to put God first. Now they do more business in six days than any other fast-food company does in seven days. I love the fact that, on any given Sunday, Mr. Cathy wasn't hustling in the home office or traveling to see the world. No, he was in the house of God serving teenagers by leading a

Sunday school class. What a legacy he left in the earth by honoring and valuing God on the Sabbath day!

Many today don't believe it's necessary to honor a sabbath day and are doing things how they want. A lot of people don't believe there is value in being connected in a local church faithfully, but studies have shown that there are many benefits—better marriages, more sense of purpose, more fulfillment, lower stress levels, and even a longer life. A study conducted at the University of Vanderbilt was showcased in several news platforms around the US. It reported as follows: "Our findings support the overall hypothesis that increased religiosity—as determined by attendance at worship services—is associated with less stress and enhanced longevity."[9] The study revealed that those who attend worship services regularly have less stress, and cut their mortality rate by 55 percent.

Many are experiencing lack of fulfillment, stress, anxiety, exhaustion, and burnout—so why would anyone add more? I am not suggesting that we add more. I am saying we reorder what is important according to God's Word. We need to redeem the time, or put it back in order, with God at the top, not the bottom—let alone when He's not even on the list. We need to do less of the good things that aren't the best things. We need to honor a sabbath day of rest to focus on God's house: His presence, people, and purpose.

---

9 Marino A, Bruce, et al., "Church Attendance, Allostatic Load and Mortality in Middle Aged Adults," *PloS One*, Public Library of Science, 16 May 2017, https://www.ncbi.nlm.nih.gov/pmc/articles/PMC5433740/.

This doesn't mean don't do anything on the Sabbath. It means don't just go about your normal routine. We have six days for that, but this day is set apart. Exodus 20:9-10 (NLT) explains: "You have six days each week for your ordinary work, but the seventh day is a Sabbath day of rest dedicated to the LORD your God." This means I use my energy less on the Sabbath by limiting what I commit to. It is a day in which I *recharge* my body and my emotions. When we get physically drained, it leads to emotional and spiritual fatigue. This becomes chronic as we work longer hours, have more to manage, sleep less, and exercise less. We wear busyness like a badge, but God says that's not wise. Every week, we are to stop and pause to rest in the world we have created in our lives with our family of origin and choice.

It's not a law; it's a principle. It's strategic. If you will do it God's way, you will do it better and longer. A great question to ask yourself is, "What do I need to stop?" Regardless of what most believe, the answer isn't to stop connecting in corporate worship. You can't prove that using Scripture. Understand what the Lord wants you to do, and do it.

I've always encouraged our church after the service to go have a great meal, connect, laugh, and rest. Take a nap, and dare your kids to wake you up. Stop the grind, and renew your body and emotions. I know you may feel guilty, but just keep your eyes on honoring God and know He is always pleased with this kind of faith.

The second benefit of sabbath is *I renew my spirit*. In the book of Matthew, Jesus told people not to worry so much. You can't change anything with your worry, but your worship can change everything.

Living a God-first life and doing things His way causes all things to be added to my life, including renewal. Matthew 6:33 (ESV) says, "But seek first the kingdom of God and his righteousness, and all these things will be added to you."

All worry leads to anxiety, so stop using energy on other things. Instead, honor God, and practice sabbath to turn your worry into worship. We tend to pull away from others—God, church, worship—and that is never the answer. On a Sunday morning, you unplug to come to church and hear from God—you stop the noise of life and embrace your place in His presence, with His people, living out His purpose. You lean in to worship God and open your heart to hear His Word taught. The whole family is renewed, and God adds peace, faith, joy, love, and every other good thing to your lives. You may come in tired, weak, challenged, and doubtful, but then God speaks into your spirit, breathes into your spirit, and it's like oxygen to your soul! This is why you need it weekly! Start off your week putting God first.

Lastly, honoring a sabbath will refocus my purpose. It reminds me of what is really important. It reminds us that, even when things on earth don't work out the way we want, earth isn't our destiny. Heaven is. Even if we have neglected the Sabbath or made mistakes, God doesn't just angrily rebuke us. He comes down and gives us a renewed and refocused purpose.

Get eyes off you, and get them back on Jesus. If You have a pulse, you have a purpose. You were made to make an eternal difference in the lives of people. It doesn't mean you won't have pain or problems, but you will focus on purpose and those who are hurting. Bring the truth back into focus. Your purpose and Your God are bigger than your problems! Your problem may seem too big for you, but it's just the right size for God.

No matter how overwhelmed you may feel, God wants to speak to you—to speak over your life. He comes to you in your desert and says, "I've got you. I have a plan for you. I am still with you and for you. I'm not going to leave you or give up on you. You will come out of this! It's not over."

God has the final say in your life and your purpose. When we commit to honoring God and the Sabbath, we will turn our worry into worship, and that changes everything, every time. It's God's plan to help us run our race with endurance to the end and finish strong! It doesn't matter how you started—only how you finish! Why don't you get planted in God's house, so you can flourish, finish strong, and enjoy the journey?

FOLLOW THE LEADER

STAY CONNECTED